The Positive Pianist

The Positive Pianist

How Flow Can Bring Passion to Practice and Performance

Thomas J. Parente

OXFORD
UNIVERSITY PRESS

OXFORD
UNIVERSITY PRESS

Oxford University Press is a department of the University of
Oxford. It furthers the University's objective of excellence in research,
scholarship, and education by publishing worldwide.

Oxford   New York
Auckland   Cape Town   Dar es Salaam   Hong Kong   Karachi
Kuala Lumpur   Madrid   Melbourne   Mexico City   Nairobi
New Delhi   Shanghai   Taipei   Toronto

With offices in
Argentina   Austria   Brazil   Chile   Czech Republic   France   Greece
Guatemala   Hungary   Italy   Japan   Poland   Portugal   Singapore
South Korea   Switzerland   Thailand   Turkey   Ukraine   Vietnam

Oxford is a registered trademark of Oxford University Press
in the UK and certain other countries.

Published in the United States of America by
Oxford University Press
198 Madison Avenue, New York, NY 10016

© Oxford University Press 2015

Library of Congress Cataloging-in-Publication Data
Parente, Thomas J.
The positive pianist: how flow can bring passion to practice and performance /
Thomas J. Parente.
  pages cm
Includes bibliographical references and index. ISBN 978–0–19–931659–5
(cloth: alk. paper) — ISBN 978–0–19–931660–1 (pbk. : alk. paper)
1. Piano—Instruction and study.   2. Piano—Performance—
Psychological aspects.   I. Title.
MT220.P24 2015
786.2'193—dc23
2014026936

9 8 7 6 5 4 3 2 1
Printed in the United States of America
on acid-free paper

To my teacher and mentor Ann Schein

CONTENTS

FOREWORD

Body, mind, and the ineffable artistic spirit all come together in the intriguing and extraordinarily fulfilling act of playing classical music well at the piano. Many people, dreaming of this fulfillment, take up the study of the piano with diligence, only to find a certain frustration and tedium when it comes to daily practicing. This can lead to a lingering sense of unfinished business that can last for a lifetime.

Books abound that discuss how one should practice correctly and efficiently; the subject has been well-traveled territory for generations. Such books occasionally turn out to be just a bit preachy, and even though the advice they contain can seem to make good sense, it doesn't always translate into resounding or encouraging success at the piano bench.

Thomas Parente enters this arena with a contribution that is very new, very real, and not quite like anything we've seen before. With down-to-earth candor, he integrates powerful principles from the fields of learning theory and psychology into piano practicing in a remarkably clear, inspiring, engaging, and pragmatic way. His ideas are based on thorough research and solid practice.

The stages of mastery outlined by Paul Fitts and Michael Posner are absolutely appropriate to piano playing and are applied by Parente understandably and entertainingly. Parente goes a bit farther and integrates, seamlessly, the wonderfully inspiring notion of the "flow" state, as defined by the groundbreaking work of Mihaly Csikszentmihalyi. Not only does Parente possess the gift of making all these theoretical ideas accessible and practical, but it all leads to what makes his approach so distinctive, namely, the conviction that what we can expect every day in the practice room is not only achievement but also something much more profound: joy, fun, delight, and the blissful absorption in a productive activity that is the hallmark of the "flow" experience in any aspect of life. This is indeed more satisfaction than many piano students, at all levels of expertise and experience, have ever dared to hope for.

William Westney

Author, *The Perfect Wrong Note:*

Learning to Trust Your Musical Self

ACKNOWLEDGMENTS

I never teach my pupils; I only attempt to provide the conditions in which they can learn.
Albert Einstein

The greatest measure of gratitude must be given to my loving wife, Dr. Susan Parente, without whose support writing this book would not have been possible. Sue, you have been my guiding light and the perfect partner—loving, encouraging, patient, and supportive in ways that you may not realize. Gifted clinical psychologist that you are, you have not only provided much-needed emotional support through the writing of both my dissertation and now this book but also greatly enhanced my understanding of the scholarship and literature on mindfulness and positive psychology. Who could ask for a better partner?

Further gratitude goes to my adviser at Teachers College, Columbia, Dr. Lori Custodero, for her guidance through my doctoral dissertation, which directly led to the writing of this book.

And I wish to thank my instructors at Teachers College, including the late great pedagogues Dino Anagnost and Robert Pace, both of whom exuded musicianship and artistry of the highest caliber. Thank you for your inspiration and the questioning attitude toward teaching and learning that you have provided.

Thank you to the thousands of students (both inside and outside Westminster Choir College of Rider University) whom I have taught over the years. In an interesting way, our roles have become somewhat reversed. I have learned so much from your efforts, accomplishments, suggestions, smiles, occasional tears, and subtle exhortations for greater scholarship that I may more fully and continually embody the honored title of *educator*, a word whose roots come from the Latin meaning "to lead out." I now believe more than ever that leading the student outward, using his or her innate abilities and strengths, from ignorance to knowledge and mastery is at the very core of what we should do as teachers.

To my son, Danny, and my daughter, Andrea: you exude so many great qualities that I am frankly in awe of. Danny, you are becoming the musician for this millennium—gifted Rutgers master's degree student in bassoon performance, pianist, rock bassist, composer, and arranger. Wow! Andrea, you are the best daughter a father could hope for. You're a gifted violinist, and your current path to a Rutgers bachelor's degree in philosophy is sure to benefit our planet upon graduation. You're the best!

To my wonderful editors Timothy DeWerff, Todd Waldman, my sister Debra Parente-Rosin, Norman Hirschy of Oxford University Press, and Production Editor Molly Morrison of Newgen: your constant exhortations for excellence were a bar worth striving for. I could not have done this without you.

To my parents and Aunt Liz: although you are no longer with us, I know that you are smiling—somewhere. You did well!

I would finally like to thank my many wonderful piano teachers and mentors and my cherished readers. Absorbing, adapting, and modifying my teachers' approaches to learning have uniquely influenced the thoughts contained in this book. Likewise, a key to attaining flow will be the adaptation and modification of my ideas contained here to fit your own learning style. Once flow is discovered and honored, it can provide the foundation necessary for the emergence of a true artistry—one that is free and fully satisfying.

Tom

ABOUT THE COMPANION WEBSITE

www.oup.com/us/thepositivepianist

A word on the website, and its videos, that accompany chapter 6: It is my fond hope that the viewing of these examples will ignite your own ideas regarding practice decisions. Viewed as a model for imitation or adaptation (however radical!), may they stimulate curiosity into personal practice procedures that eventually will lead you into the marvelous state of flow. Please don't be a stranger! I look forward to your thoughts, reactions, and questions should you wish to voice them. Throughout the text, audio clips are signaled by this symbol: ▶.

The Positive Pianist

CHAPTER 1

Loving What You Do, Doing What You Love

Art enables us to find ourselves and lose ourselves at the same time.
Thomas Merton

Thirty-five years ago on a hot July day, I drove from northern New Jersey to upstate New York with my fiancée to visit my grandmother. Although I did not realize it at the time, that visit was to have a lasting influence on my approach to music, for it was during this visit that my grandmother, the daughter of southern Italian immigrants, was to share with me her philosophy of life. It is only now that I realize that for all of the ensuing years, I have been testing the ins and outs and the nooks and crannies of her simple wisdom. I say "simple" because, until recently, I viewed it as such. However, having read many books and articles over the years and eventually attaining a doctorate along the way related to this subject, I now realize that hers was a philosophy strong enough to serve as a lifelong guidepost.

It was in her kitchen, while my future wife and I were sipping her homemade lemonade and eating Italian pastries, that my grandmother told us that the key to happiness is to love what you are doing. Perplexed, I asked, "Even if it is something you don't like to do, like sweeping the floor?" "Yes," she answered, "for the love of doing it will ensure that it gets done right." Still skeptical, I told her that I didn't think it was possible: "If I don't like sweeping the floor, how can I possibly learn to love doing it?" "It's easy," she answered. "Just don't think of anything else, and notice what you're doing."

I have often thought about her words and wondered whether they could be applied to all situations, in particular to my work as a pianist and piano teacher. Since becoming aware of the concept of flow nearly twenty years ago when I read *Finding Flow* by Mihaly Csikszentmihalyi (1997), I have come to believe in the power of my grandmother's words. Csikszentmihalyi led me to understand that even the simple tasks performed by a goatherd or a farmer could provide a peak experience of enjoyment and full concentration—better known as flow. At that time, I was also reminded of the advice in the book *Be Here Now* (1971) by Ram Dass, who encouraged full and unmitigated attention as a path to heightened awareness. His and Csikszentmihalyi's writings seemed like good advice if one had to sweep the floor or herd goats. However, was this "love what you do" idea applicable to something as complex as learning to play the piano?

As a teacher who believed in being open to new ideas and ways of doing things, I was extremely curious. Despite Csikszentmihalyi's assertion that chess masters, composers, athletes, and even top surgeons went into flow and credited much of their success to being in this state, I still had my doubts, despite the fact that as a Dalcroze eurhythmics teacher of small children, I had frequently experienced the flow state, as had my students. As a practitioner of Dalcroze eurhythmics (the prefix *eu-* is from the Greek meaning "good," and *rhythmos* coincidentally and significantly means "flow"), I had gradually grown accustomed to experiencing many of the characteristics of flow. What was compelling upon first contact with the Dalcroze method and continues to this day is the sheer joy that often occurs in a eurhythmics class for everyone involved, myself very much included. My own students concur with this statement as they often relate how pleasurable they found the experience. I learned later that the presence of the flow state in children had been the topic of research conducted by Dr. Lori Custodero of Teachers College, Columbia University, who had developed an observational tool for measuring flow in children. Whether being in flow could aid in learning the piano was of vital importance to me, since as a pianist and private and group piano teacher, I was personally invested in learning the answer to this most fundamental of questions. I had an additional sense of urgency, since I had come to the piano not as a child, as had most of my fellow pianists, but far later. With a lot of catching up to do, I was intrigued by an idea: imagine what one might be capable of learning at the piano if "love what you do" were indeed the secret not only to life but also to learning a Bach fugue! I am now convinced that finding ways to ignite passion for piano practicing is something we seldom think about but that is, nevertheless, essential to our growth as artists.

I first heard the word *ignition* when I was eight years old. I remember distinctly the utter excitement as the world waited for pioneering astronaut John Glenn to take off in his little space capsule in order to orbit around the earth. Here was something new and electrifying. The very words *ignition* and *liftoff* were new and exciting—at least to me. To this day, they have always been associated with the John Glenn adventure. Which comes first, ignition or liftoff? Does one need to be ignited in order to be lifted? Or does the lift itself create the ignition? Clearly, in the case of Glenn and every vehicle that is launched either horizontally or vertically, ignition precedes the launch. However, it would seem that in the case of a developing artist, these two concepts are deliciously intermingled. Or they should be.

Igniting the imagination in attempting to "launch" or give full expression to the soul is the desire of every artist, whether he or she has reached the elite status or is a beginner. Practitioners of Zen would have us believe that every master must have the spirit of the beginner. So if this is the case, then where do ignition and launching come in?

We in the artistic world must always contend with the terror of beginnings, whether the beginning of a new semester (something I am facing as I type these very words), the blank page that begins a writing project, or the question of how one begins when sitting down to practice the piano. Beginnings are always difficult, yet Zen masters consistently contend that in order to be free, one must have the uncluttered mind of the beginner. What a paradox. In order to access the soul, we must be willing to embrace the less enjoyable experience that one encounters at the beginning of a project. The terror of the blank page over and over and over again. It sounds like one of the rings that Dante described in his *Inferno*. However, if we look at beginnings with the curiosity and freshness of a young child (John Glenn again returns to mind), we will gradually free ourselves from the feeling of arduousness that often accompanies the act of sitting down to practice.

Yet the purity of the beginning mind and the seemingly stimulating, perhaps even exciting, notion of ignition leading to launch are not incompatible. There is a famous story told by Robert Craft—the composer, theorist, and assistant to Igor Stravinsky—regarding Stravinsky's writing of *Le sacre du printemps* (*The Rite of Spring*). According to Craft, Stravinsky claimed to have been in something of a trance while composing the piece, during which time his pen seemed to move of its own volition. The altered state of mind that Stravinsky so aptly described put him in touch with something that was far deeper than the norm. He obviously tapped into something that drove his genius:

> I was guided by no system whatever in *Le sacre du printemps*. When I think of the other composers of that time who interest me—Berg, who is synthetic (in the best sense), Webern, who is analytic, and Schoenberg, who is both—how much more theoretical their music seems than *Le sacre*; and these composers were supported by a great tradition, whereas very little immediate tradition lies behind *Le sacre du printemps*. I had only my ear to help me. I heard and I wrote what I heard. I am the vessel through which *Le sacre* passed.
>
> (Stravinsky and Craft 1962, 147–48)

Johannes Brahms seems to have experienced a similar state when composing:

> I am in a trance-like condition—hovering between being asleep and awake; I am still conscious but right on the border of losing consciousness, and it is at such moments that inspired ideas come.
>
> (quoted in Abell, 1987, 9)

Richard Strauss seemed to agree:

> When in my most inspired moods, I have definite compelling visions, involving a higher selfhood. I feel at such moments that I am tapping the source of infinite and Eternal energy from which you and I and all things proceed.
>
> (quoted in Abell 1987, 98)

I, too, can remember a time when the excitement and the joy of making music prevailed without any hindrance coming from fear. I also remember the lesson in which potential embarrassment or fear began to encroach on this unrestrained joy that I felt while sitting at the piano. Since I had not had many years of consistent piano lessons from an experienced piano teacher (my piano teacher was primarily a singer and could not play himself), I was really never given a firm foundation. I now recall with amusement that my interpretation of rhythmic values was based merely on my impressions of when to play fast or slow. Hence, if there was more visual space in the measure, the notes would be longer. If there was less space in the measure, that surely meant that those notes took less time. The values that had doubled beams, which I would later learn are called sixteenth notes, were clearly meant to be played as fast as possible. You get the picture. Armed with my own somewhat impressionistic sense of timing, I embarked on the first movement of Clementi's Second Sonatina. I remember playing with gusto and with lots of energy.

Finally, the day of my piano lesson arrived—a day I eagerly awaited given my passionate rendering of the Clementi. It was a Saturday, so my father was home and, of course, watching the Yankees game (we were both avid New York Yankees fans). The fact that I was to have a piano lesson in the room on the other side of the wall was of no consequence, since keeping track of the team and the statistics that go along with tracking baseball had Talmudic intensity in the Parente household. The doorbell rang at the stroke of three. As usual, my piano teacher was exactly punctual in his arrival. I ran to the door and greeted him while the strains of "Take Me Out to the Ballgame" issued from my parents' bedroom. Undeterred, I was eager to play my newly learned Clementi for him.

I sat down and began. It seemed to be going really well, and I was very proud of myself. I finished as if the curtain had just closed on Verdi's *La forza del destino*. When I finished, my teacher fell silent. Normally a garrulous, charming man (he had emigrated from Italy about fifteen years before and still had Italianate joie de vivre), he had been struck speechless. After a few seconds of silence (while not complete, actually, since I could still hear that the Yankees were batting in the bottom of the eighth), he said two words: *"Why, Tom?"* I had no idea what he was asking me until I looked at his face, which was a mixture of dismay and disappointment tinged with, I later realized, anger. I remember being sincerely perplexed, as I had worked so hard and with such gusto. But I had obviously let my piano teacher down, and I really didn't know what to do.

Fortunately, at that very moment, I heard my dad cheer as Joe Pepitone (himself an Italian-American) hit a homer. Within a second, my father raced out of the bedroom, oblivious to the drama that had just taken place, to shake my hand, which was a ritual we did every time a Yankee hit a homer. My piano teacher's face turned from dismay, disappointment, and a little anger to complete bewilderment. After my dad returned to watching the game, I explained that this was significant because Pepitone was Italian, a random statement that, of course, had nothing to do with the piano lesson (actually, I missed an opportunity to connect Pepitone to Clementi since both were Italian, which would have been another random observation but might have dispelled some of the heaviness of the moment). After the very confusing and chaotic five minutes that had just passed, I remember feeling an emotion that was entirely unfamiliar. Unfortunately, a very important and rather sad seed had been planted, for this was the first time I began to associate potential embarrassment with my pianistic efforts. What had been a source of pride was now a source of embarrassment and even shame.

Brené Brown, the author of *Daring Greatly: How the Courage to Be Vulnerable Transforms the Way We Live, Love, Parent, and Lead* (2012), contends that shame brings about fear and disengagement. Disengagement in turn destroys creativity, learning, and innovation. Yet encounters of the type I have described permeate the piano teaching profession. When I was a student at the Manhattan School of Music, several of my fellow students would leave their lessons crying because of the destructive attitudes of their teachers. I distinctly recall several students telling me a variation of the same story, in which the teacher, after listening to the student, would say something along the lines of "You call yourself a musician, how *dare* you?" The pedagogical technique of shaming a student may have a short-term consequence of increasing practice time, but it does nothing for the individual artist who is yearning to emerge. For if students get the message that their sincere efforts are unworthy of their teachers, then they are most likely left with idea that their musical spirit does not count.

Going back to my episode with the Clementi, there clearly were many problems with my interpretation that day (I frankly shudder when I think back). However, these infelicities were nothing when compared with the hit my self-esteem took that afternoon from my teacher's reaction. The issues with my playing that were admittedly less than ideal could have been dealt with in a systematic manner that left my love for the Clementi completely intact. Instead, as is too often present during the piano teacher-student relationship, blame and shame were directed toward me instead of solid teaching and intervention. As the vast majority of students in such a position experience, I felt vulnerable and unable to remedy the situation.

The great question that perplexes all artists, no matter where they are on the continuum of proficiency, is how to retain our individuality and the spark of life that animates our love of the art, while taking the steps that are necessary to develop greater skill. Most often, skill development becomes reminiscent of the doctor who advises you to take the bitter medicine since "it will be good for you." So many of us have acquiesced to this notion of life that the doors to our souls, which once were open, gradually close. To paraphrase this great question, how do we maintain the "love" during learning? As we will discover in the coming chapters, the path is clear, and we already have the answer. Really, we do!

Over the past four years, my search for the answer has intensified, leading me to a more thorough study of the literature on flow as I have pursued my doctorate at Teachers College, Columbia University. In conjunction with this research, I have discovered that "teaching to flow" is a compelling way both to energize my teaching and to enable my private students and secondary pianists—students for whom piano is not their main instrument—to learn in a way that is relatively conflict-free, even joyful. I have found that the more I teach to flow as an organizing principle, the greater the achievements of my students. I have also learned that the best way to lead students to flow is through teaching awareness of flow characteristics and encouraging student collaboration.

The Positive Pianist: How Flow Can Bring Passion to Practice and Performance draws on my forty years of teaching and research to show piano students and their teachers how to draw on every student's natural curiosity and drive for mastery to develop the proper mental attitude and focus for practicing the piano. Through achieving a state of total concentration—or flow—the student is able to give full attention to the art of practicing and make the kinds of moment-to-moment decisions that positively affect every aspect of music making. The book shows not only how the practice session can be organized to optimize the emergence of the flow state but also how the flow state, once achieved, can provide both optimal learning conditions and musical enjoyment. Throughout the book, I attempt to provide students with the ability to make small, intermediate, and grand decisions that are well suited to their ability at any given moment. Since the goal is to attain optimal learning conditions (or flow), central to this strategy will be the notion that pianists' moment-to-moment psychological, musical, and physical reactions are to be trusted and acted upon so they may learn how to use this information while they practice to enhance their musical experience.

To that end, I provide in this book an overview of useful insights and techniques for manipulating conditions so that you, as a student or as a teacher, may experience the optimal experience of flow. This includes a description of the flow state and a discussion of how striving for flow positively affects both practicing and overall learning. In addition to teaching about flow, I have found that describing the various stages of learning and skill acquisition that my students will traverse on their way to mastery provides them with a blueprint by which they can chart their progress.

I have also found essential the model of classical learning stages offered by skills-acquisition researchers Paul M. Fitts and Michael I. Posner in their book *Human Performance* (1967). This model, called "phases of learning," simultaneously provides students with a procedural blueprint while enabling them to become more accepting of their individual rates of progress. This self-acceptance is key, since pianists' awareness of individual differences in how we learn makes them more patient and understanding of the various stages we all must go through on the way to learning a skill. During this discussion, I also attempt to tie learning stages to Csikszentmihalyi's and Custodero's descriptions of flow characteristics.

It is my hope that you will gain the courage to honor the artist within you. It has been a guiding principle of mine ever since I began teaching forty years ago that each of us possesses a unique spirit or genius that, given the right circumstances and experiences, has the capacity to contribute something unique to humanity—be it great or small. Honoring your inner artist as a learner will mean to insist that each time you sit down to practice, you will do so in a manner that can give rise to optimal experience or flow. As a teacher, it will mean to charge yourself to treat each student as an emerging artist and to create an atmosphere in which enjoyment of the piano and mutual respect may flourish. It means that both student and teacher will become collaborators in their pursuit of musical growth.

CHAPTER 2

Flow Experience

We have all experienced times when, instead of being buffeted by anonymous forces, we do feel in control of our actions, masters of our own fate. On the rare occasions that it happens, we feel a sense of exhilaration, a deep sense of enjoyment that is long cherished and that becomes a landmark in memory for what life should be like.

Mihaly Csikszentmihalyi

FLOW AND MOTIVATION

Mihaly Csikszentmihalyi, the author of the above quotation (1975), is responsible for the term *flow* as it relates to human psychology. The flow state he described, a "sense of exhilaration" and "deep sense of enjoyment," may be experienced by participants in any number of pursuits. Those who experience flow have usually chosen to take part in the activity for the sheer joy of doing it, not from any expectation of reward. You can probably think of a number of times when you have experienced such a feeling. Perhaps it was while you were enjoying gardening, exercising, reading, shopping, or skiing. These are the times when you are most likely to be unaware of the passage of time.

When we do something for the simple love of doing it, we are intrinsically motivated to do it. When *intrinsic* factors are not present, then *extrinsic* factors often become the engines behind the action. The wide array of extrinsic factors include performing an activity in order to do the following.

Receive praise. We all crave praise from any quarter. Adulation from friends, colleagues, bosses, professional associates, and even strangers can make our day and validate our worth. Craving such attention has the potential of motivating us to extreme effort, since our self-esteem may depend on it.

Be paid or receive a reward. A 2011 Conference Review Board survey reported that well more than half of Americans are unhappy with their jobs and thus get up and go to work solely for the extrinsic benefit of being paid. We all have to earn enough money to live, but only the most fortunate among us are able to find work that can provide inner fulfillment while paying the bills. In your own circle of friends, think of the many people you know who would seek some other employment if they were able to maintain their lifestyle by working at a job they really enjoyed.

Impress friends and acquaintances. We all wish to be held in high esteem by our peers, and doing something that will earn respect and admiration from a friend or acquaintance can propel us to act.

Satisfy a teacher. A student's fondness for a teacher may spur the student to work especially hard, since the student knows that such action may gratify the teacher. This observation is all too common. Rosy Martin writes in *Phototherapy: The School Photograph* (1986), "The good schoolgirl, the academic achiever, was the part of me that sought solace in pleasing the teacher." Inevitably, there is often a downside: "However, I was constantly anxious, afraid both of failure and success, a perfectionist, who always managed to get something wrong." It is clear that this student is not performing an action for the love of it.

Satisfy one's parents. Until the all-but-inevitable adolescent rift occurs between child and parent, satisfying one's parents can be a powerful motivator of a child's actions, whether it is doing homework, brushing teeth, or practicing an instrument. In some cultures, the entire process of socialization is tied to pleasing one's parents. Children from these cultures are motivated by their society to please their parents with a sense of duty. It has been my experience that when students who have been strictly acculturated to please their parents are given the liberty to live their lives free from their parents' scrutiny and to please themselves, they often go to the other extreme, becoming lazy, lethargic, and unmotivated to do just about anything, let alone practice an instrument.

Extrinsic motivators, such as those cited here, are therefore inferior as driving forces. If one were to remove the praise, reward, or parent/teacher involvement, the activity would most likely no longer be undertaken.

Avoiding punishment is also a powerful extrinsic motivator. In the case of the piano student, avoiding embarrassment or a teacher's harsh words can fall into this category. In his autobiography, famed pianist Lang Lang recounts the abusive yelling and insults he had to endure from one of his teachers, whom he renamed "Professor Angry": "Even when

I was absolutely convinced that I had mastered a difficult Schubert or Tchaikovsky piece Professor Angry sat there unimpressed. [She] was never satisfied." Lang Lang talks about practicing until his fingers ached in order to satisfy and avoid his teacher's harsh criticism.

When, as a young man, the soon-to-be-great pianist Ignaz Friedman first began lessons with legendary pianist and teacher Theodor Leschetizky, he was told by the great master, "Don't bother with the piano, you will most likely play the tuba better (Evans 2009, 30)." Leschetizky dealt with Benno Moiseiwitsch, another of his pupils, in a similar manner. After Moiseiwitsch had finished playing for him for the first time, Leschetizky uttered a scathing critique: "Well, I could play better with my feet than that" (*ibid.*). Moiseiwitsch commented many years later that he suspected that this was Leschetizky's way of bringing him down initially so he could then build him back up in his own image. Avoidance of such criticism initially became a powerful motivator for both Friedman and Moiseiwitsch and later for Lang Lang during their early careers. However, what undoubtedly sustained and guided these three pianistic giants to rise above their teachers' harsh words was their great talent and love for the piano.

In the world of the virtuoso, such stories are quite common, and one has to applaud the fortitude of those who can prosper in the face of such criticism. Much more common, however, is the student who comes home and tells her mom that she just "can't do anything right." Or the student who is deliberately and repeatedly demeaned by the teacher in the Leschetizky-like hope that the student will rise to the occasion and "shape up." Too often, one hears stories such as the following: "The piano teacher was mean. . . . I really enjoyed the piano, but because of her I never took to it. I still believe I could have been good at it." The girl who said that went on to describe how she would even pray at bedtime that her teacher wouldn't punish her when she lost her temper. Inevitably, avoiding punishment leads to resignation, which can lead finally and most unfortunately to quitting (Martin 1986, 41).

Extrinsic motivators are ultimately counterproductive, since they can detract from the enjoyment that might have been derived from the activity were it not for the resentment that builds up when we are being forced to do something. Thus, when someone studies the piano for the sake of an extrinsic benefit alone, the result can be a lack of enjoyment and, perhaps even more important, the *expectation* of no enjoyment. In 1949, motivation researcher Harry Harlow conducted a now-famous study in which he placed two relatively complex puzzles in a cage with rhesus monkeys. The goal was to see how the monkeys would react and to test their ability to make progress in solving the puzzles. Harlow was amazed to find that the monkeys actually appeared to become fascinated by the challenge. This fascination led to a great motivation to solve the puzzles, which they did in two weeks. What made the result even more astonishing to Harlow, however, was that the motivation to solve the puzzle was not a reward such as food. In fact, when the monkeys were later rewarded (Harlow wanted to see whether he could accelerate the monkeys' speed in solving the puzzles), the opposite actually occurred. Surprisingly, they began to lose interest, and their execution speed slow down (Harlow, Harlow, and Meyer 1950).

Twenty years later, in 1969, a graduate student in psychology named Edward Deci tried a similar experiment (Deci was destined to become a major leading expert in the study of intrinsic motivation). He was curious to learn how a similar experiment would affect humans. He placed two groups of college students in rooms with several magazines and a puzzle similar to a Rubik's Cube. One group was offered payment for solving the puzzle, and the other group was simply asked to play with the puzzle. As expected, the first group worked extremely hard to solve the problem. What came next is especially interesting. The day after the experiment, Deci invited both groups back. This time, he told the first group that there was not enough money left to pay them for solving the problem. This group responded by losing interest in the task. Members of the second group, the one that was never offered money, actually spent more time with the puzzle than they had before. Thus, the presence and then absence of payment detracted from the first group's motivation for the task. However, the fascination with the puzzle fed on itself and provided motivation for further exploration for the second group. These two experiments demonstrate that engagement in an intrinsically enjoyable act can be stymied by the introduction of an extrinsic reward. This, of course, also pertains to playing the piano. The joy of playing must be the main motivator.

Individuals simply learn better when motivated to do so for intrinsic reasons—that is, for the love of doing it—since the better one becomes at performing a task, the more one wishes to do it. Thus, a "virtuous circle" is created, as the motivation to grow fuels growth, which in turn motivates further desire to grow, and so on. Can you think of any artists, entertainers, or sports figures who excelled at their craft yet didn't love what they were doing? In the words of Deci, people possess an "inherent tendency to seek out novelty and challenges, to extend and exercise their capacities, to explore, and to learn" (Deci and Ryan 2000, 70). This is why we should play the piano.

FLOW AND ITS CHARACTERISTICS

As I have already mentioned, in his many books and articles on the subject, research psychologist Mihaly Csikszentmihalyi wrote about the happiness of individuals whose intrinsic motivation drove them to participate in some activity. His exploration into the rewards that people experience while participating in enjoyable pursuits led him to study the psychological state that occurred during these periods. Many of those he interviewed used the word *flow* to describe the feeling they had while totally immersed in an activity. Statements such as "things began to flow" or "go with the flow" led him to choose the word *flow* to describe this feeling. Over the years, he was able to identify several characteristics that are present when one is in flow:

1. **The challenge being engaged in is at a level slightly above that of the individual's skill level.**

   Flow can arise when one is participating in an enjoyable activity, such as games and sports, that makes use of a high level of motor skills. Playing soccer against a much better team can be a frustrating experience; against a much weaker team, it can lead to boredom. If the members of both teams are to have a chance of experiencing flow, then neither team should be far better or worse than the other.

2. **There is a high level of concentration leading to the exclusion of extraneous thoughts such as worry or concern.**

   The basketball or hockey player becomes so engaged in the game that her awareness is fully occupied by the events unfolding on the basketball court or the ice rink. The master calligrapher is fully at one with the action of drawing his pen across the paper. An actor has become the character he is portraying. This merging of action and awareness has been made possible by clarity of the goal and by the close match between the challenge presented and the skill needed to meet it. Distractions exert no influence on the action. The concentration of the placekicker in football or the basketball player preparing to take a free throw is unaffected by the screaming fans or the effect of his actions on the game's outcome.

3. **Goals are clear.**

   There are clear goals every step of the way. In contrast to a daily routine in which one may be uncertain about what to do next, a person in flow has a clear sense of immediate and long-term goals. The painter knows precisely where to place the next brushstroke, and the writer is acutely aware of the rightness of a sentence, verse, or lyric. The surgeon knows precisely how the operation should proceed, and the master chess player intuits the long-term consequences of moving a pawn.

4. **There is no fear of failure or losing control.**

   The task that one chooses is manageable and technically solvable. Thus, one never feels out of control. Having banished all extraneous thoughts, one is so consumed with what one is doing that one ignores everything outside the action being performed. One is secure enough in one's actions that there is no fear of failure. The pitcher on the mound feels that, for this game, at least, he can rely on his curveball to nip the outside corner of the plate. The quarterback behind the line of scrimmage is certain that he can pinpoint his passes to receivers despite the fury of the oncoming tackles. The fencer never fears a sudden loss of balance, and the third rower in crew is in perfect rhythm with the other members of her boat. Her mastery leads her never to doubt her ability to stay in sync with the others.

5. **Self-consciousness diminishes or disappears.**

   One's sense of self, also extraneous to the action, disappears. "Afterwards, we may emerge with a stronger self-concept because we know that we have succeeded in meeting a difficult challenge. Paradoxically, the self expands through acts of self-forgetfulness" (Csikszentmihalyi 1997). When one is in flow, fear of embarrassment or humiliation disappears, because the voices of self-doubt have disappeared. Self-aggrandizing thoughts will also disappear, for they, too, have nothing to do with the action being performed.

6. **One's perception of time becomes altered.**

   The expression "Time flies when you're having fun" comes into play here. One cannot believe how much time elapsed while one was in flow. This phenomenon is commonly experienced by dancers, musicians, and athletes who have become so involved in what they are doing that they have lost a sense of the passage of time. Csikszentmihalyi says it clearly: "The sense of time becomes distorted. Generally in flow we forget time, and hours may pass by in what seem like a few minutes. Or the opposite happens: A figure skater may report that a quick turn lasting only a second in real time seems to stretch out for much longer. Our sense of how much time passes depends on what we are doing" (1997). Flow and a distorted sense of the passage of time often go hand in hand, and when they are absent, one may realize, that one's time has not been used as productively as it might have been.

7. **Action and awareness merge.**

   Being in flow is to be completely absorbed in an activity. In everyday experience, the mind is often disconnected from what one is doing; it's as though one were operating on autopilot. While attending a concert or a play, one's mind may wander to thoughts entirely divorced from what is happening onstage. While attending a lecture, one may hear something that is so compelling that a stream of consciousness takes over and leads one far away from the words of the speaker.

BENEFITS OF FLOW

When we are in flow, we are at our best, since all our resources unite to focus on the task at hand. Being in flow while practicing has additional benefits, in that motivation to practice will increase. This phenomenon is referred to by flow researchers as "emergent motivation." It describes how the motivation to persist in or return to an activity arises out of the enjoyment associated with the experience itself. In this way, the flow experience becomes a force for expansion in relation to the pianist's overall goals. What is crucial here is that the high quality of the activity experienced will most likely lead to behavior that is *intrinsically* motivated. If we have experienced something wonderful, we wish to experience it again and again. Each time it is experienced can lead to more fully realized goals. Thus, both the motivation to practice and the pianist's musical goals are said to be emergent as one feeds the other.

The emergent motivation associated with the flow experience fosters the development of skills. Individuals in flow thus grow in their overall ability. This is because as your skills increase, so will the challenges that you will be ready and willing to take on. A mutually reinforcing cycle thus develops, in which enjoyment leads to enhanced attention, which leads to growth in personal skills, which leads to further enjoyment.

Piano Practicing toward Flow

When you are in flow, you are in the best possible state for learning, and so you should be knowledgeable of the indicators that you are in flow while practicing. The following will help you relate your piano practice to the seven characteristics that have already been discussed.

1. **The challenge being engaged in is at a level slightly above that of the individual's skill level.**
   Playing the piano is inherently a challenging activity. In order to foster the emergence of flow while practicing, it is important to recognize

your own skill level and to work on challenges that are *just above* that skill level. This is a crucial habit to develop, for it can be tempting to choose a task that is too difficult. I will say more about this later, but the general principle is that you are better off listening to your "gut feeling" when choosing what to focus on. If it seems that the complications are too numerous and that mastery is too far away, then most likely you are attempting to accomplish something that will not yield satisfactory results in an enjoyable manner. My advice to you is simple: simplify. You can deal with the more complicated passage later, once your level of skill has increased.

2. **There is a high level of concentration leading to the exclusion of extraneous thoughts such as worry or concern.**

   Playing the piano can and should be a joyful activity. Pianists who are intensely and totally involved in their work will often report that their cares and worries seem to disappear while they are practicing. When you are totally involved in a task, there simply is no mental space for anything else. It is a rare person indeed who wouldn't be glad of a reprieve from daily cares and worries while accomplishing something worthwhile, especially if it is their life's work. The challenge is to create conditions that will be conducive to the emergence of full concentration. I will, again, discuss this at length a bit later. But for now, keep in mind that being totally involved in your practice will yield amazing results.

3. **Goals are clear.**

   When you are learning to play a piece of music, the ultimate goals are accuracy of execution and effective expression. However, to get there, you begin with the musical codes on the printed page and interpret them in a manner that leads to a gesture that in turn leads to the desired sound. Musical notation is thus akin to a Laban score for a dancer, in that explicit directions are provided on how to move. In the dancer's case, the dance movement itself is the goal. In the musician's case, the movement is not the goal but the means to the goal, which is sound.

   I observed in point 1 above that choosing tasks that you believe to be challenging yet solvable is extremely important. Being clear about your goals at all times is an important corollary to this. The goal or goals you choose must be well defined, and the solutions should be attainable (for example, your problem could be to find a fingering for a chord that enables the hand to leap to begin the following phrase).

4. **There is no fear of failure or losing control.**

   The task that one chooses should be manageable and solvable from both a technical and an expressive standpoint. As a result, you never feel about to lose control. Adjusting practice parameters, such as playing with hands together or separate, is an important consideration. Not trying to accomplish more than one challenge at a time and modifying the tempo are techniques for maintaining control consistently throughout your practice session. This may mean a change in tempo or the size of the segment you attempt (I will deal with this more thoroughly in chapter 5).

Think of the times you have sat down to practice and begun by sight-reading a passage of moderate difficulty. Pleased that the passage was easier than you thought, you read through it a few times, only to discover that little glitches crept in—a wrong note here, a cramped arm there, a less-than-robust rhythm, or a lackluster tone. Perhaps the passage wasn't as easy as your first impression led you to believe. Perhaps the complications that arose during those first attempts were simply too numerous for you to address on the fly. As a result, you may not have experienced the full level of control necessary to fully master the passage. To achieve mastery, it is essential that you choose challenges that allow for immediate control according to your musical concept.

5. **Self-consciousness diminishes or disappears.**
As noted above, when pianists are in the flow state, they are conscious only of the action that they are performing, and their awareness is completely devoted to that action. They lose their sense of self, because there is no mental energy left for anything external to the music.

Because of the all-consuming aspect of being in the flow state, you will not be concerned with how others perceive you. Freed from the burden of negative thinking, you can allow yourself to be fully "in the moment." Perhaps even more important than how others perceive you is how you perceive yourself. Thus, you will not experience such self-defeating thoughts as "I will never get this right" or "Maybe I should just give up on this piece." We all know that such thoughts are self-defeating, but stopping the onslaught of such thoughts cannot be achieved by telling yourself to "just stay positive." This loss of concern for self-image is often what people refer to when they say that they were fully "in the zone." Practicing from such a mental state will eliminate this problem. So if you have suffered from harsh self-criticism during practice, be prepared for a surprise: once you begin to experience flow, you will be so fully involved in what you are doing that you will have no mental space for that negative voice.

6. **One's perception of time becomes altered.**
The almost universal reaction to engaging fully in an enjoyable activity to feel that time seems to fly. Because of intense concentration, when you are in the state of flow, you are unaware of the passage of time.

You have likely had this experience many times while playing the piano or perhaps during another activity not related to piano practice. Maybe it occurred while you were playing a game or talking with your friends. It may have occurred while you were reading or performing onstage. Several of my students have said that they would go into the zone when they played soccer or danced. Practicing while in flow or while in the zone will result in practice sessions whose durations will be longer and longer, since the time spent will be undoubtedly far more enjoyable, resulting in more time on task.

7. Action and awareness merge.

When you become totally absorbed in playing the piano, there is a feeling that the doing and the thinking are a single activity. The great benefit of such total absorption is that you will be completely wrapped up in what you are doing. Under such conditions, learning is optimal.

Being in the flow state is to be completely engrossed in an activity. The ability to create an environment in which the flow state can flourish is of utmost importance to the piano student. Because of the all-encompassing nature of the flow state, it greatly enhances the degree of learning.

SITTING DOWN TO PRACTICE: CREATING THE RIGHT CONDITIONS

It has been my experience that during practice, students often will work in a manner that is undisciplined, unplanned, and, as a result, unfocused. The result of this "mindless" approach to studying the piano is that students are often unresponsive to the technical and musical problems that emerge during practice simply because they do not notice them. Their inattentiveness to the demands of the present moment often leads them to become distractible and hence chaotic in their learning as they move through the entire piece in a disorganized manner. Their lack of a conscious or mindful approach to their work prevents them from experiencing the enjoyment that could have been derived from fostering flow through mindful attention.

There is wide agreement that flow normally does not occur until at least twenty to thirty minutes have elapsed. This is the start-up time, when decisions regarding moment-to-moment choices are crucial. During this time, it is essential that you manage challenges that still present a modicum of unknown territory so there is no danger of becoming bored. Cultivating mindfulness during this all-important initial period will help you with the decisions necessary for success.

TOWARD MINDFUL PRACTICING

In an interview for a *Washington Post* article that explored the notion of mindfulness, Jon Kabat-Zinn, founding director of the Stress Reduction Clinic and the Center for Mindfulness in Medicine, Health Care, and Society at the University of Massachusetts Medical School and founder of Mindfulness-Based Stress Reduction (MBSR) stated: "When you pay attention to boredom, it gets unbelievably interesting" (Simon 2005).

We are thus reminded that simply being attentive can create interest and engagement. This attention must be intentional and without the self-critical and judgmental thinking that is common among pianists. Flow takes time to emerge, and being fully mindful and attentive during this initial period is a crucial component to its emergence. Mindfulness relates to the ability to be focused in the present and not have one's attention diverted by anxiety or by thoughts such as "I must work hard" or "No pain, no gain." Even thoughts such as "Now, make sure you concentrate" are antithetical to mindfulness, because they detract from attentiveness.

Lack of attention can lead to mindless behavior. According to Harvard professor Ellen Langer, who is best known for her studies on mindfulness theory, "Mindlessness . . . is characterized by automatic behavior that precludes attending to new signals. . . . Being mindless, colloquially speaking, is like being on automatic pilot" (Langer 1997, 4). When we are mindless, we are not attentive to the details of what we are doing. Too often, piano students attempt to practice without even first considering whether what they are doing is the best way to begin. This mindless, unquestioning approach invariably leads to poor learning and a repetition of a script that is likely to be counterproductive and antithetical to the emergence of flow.

A more mindful approach to practicing is just the opposite, in that the individual is attentive to details *and* to his or her own thought process. A mindful person is consumed with actions taking place in the present moment and is able to evaluate actions continually for their efficacy. Mindfulness can be considered an enhanced attention to one's present reality. When applied to practicing the piano, this enhanced attention to current actions, with the student fully engaged in the moment, can enhance the acquisition of pianistic skills.

As you attempt to be attentive to the learning process in the hope of creating conditions under which good learning may evolve, you may be stymied by making moment-to-moment decisions that are counterproductive. The discouragement that such a state can evoke often has the effect of circling you back to a familiar yet mindless approach, which, again, is not a fruitful place for flow to emerge. So in an attempt to practice in a manner conducive to the emergence of flow, try beginning your practice session with the following:

1. **Play something that gives immediate and conflict-free enjoyment.**
   For some of you, this may be scales, arpeggios, or exercises that "get the blood flowing." What is crucial here is that what you choose does not have to be one of the standard ways you may have been taught to begin your piano practice. If playing scales, arpeggios, or exercises has the effect of promoting being in the zone, then more power to you. However, for many of us, this is not an optimal first step. Perhaps improvising or playing a pop song or a light classical piece that you have fully mastered and that both speaks directly to and comes from your heart may be a better way to begin. To avoid boredom, try adding something new such as dynamic surprises or thicker textures (in the case of the pop song or improvisation), or maybe even sing along.

2. **Find a section in a piece that you are working on that has already or nearly been worked out.**
   Recall the process that brought you to your current level of mastery. Remember that you have already enjoyed success, and try to recall the process that resulted in this.

3. **You are now ready to begin to tackle something new.**
   It is advisable at this stage of learning that you attempt to learn a segment that is clearly within your capacity. The segment you choose should contain challenges that are very nearly at the same skill level, or slightly above it, you perceive yourself to be in the current moment.

   This process should take approximately twenty to thirty minutes. You may now notice that some of the flow characteristics that were discussed earlier are beginning to emerge. To see whether you are on track, ask yourself such questions as "How is my control?" or "Is my skill level well balanced to the challenge I have chosen?" If everything feels just right, then proceed accordingly. However, you may wish to modify the challenge if control is deficient or the challenge is too great.

SUMMARY

When we are in flow, we are motivated to perform an action for its intrinsic worth, that is, for the satisfaction or joy it brings; the challenge we have chosen is only slightly above our perceived skill level;

our concentration is total, and worries disappear; goals are clear; we are not fearful of losing control or of failure; self-consciousness disappears; time flies; and our doing and thinking become one. When flow is present, we are at our best, and our growth potential—our ability to learn—is at its optimal state.

People in flow experience an ever-increasing desire to do an action over and over again. This, in turn, builds skill, which causes advancement through the cycle of taking on ever-increasing challenges. The desire to practice becomes greater, thanks to the increasing success that accompanies the whole process. The maxim of success begetting success is particularly apropos here.

To foster the emergence of flow, you have to be careful during the initial period of practice, since flow takes time to emerge. Therefore, careful and mindful scaffolding of your actions, in which you avoid tasks that are far too complex, is essential for its emergence.

CHAPTER 3

Building Skills

Part of the challenge for piano students to get into flow is to recognize the motor-skills acquisition and developmental stages that they experience when learning music. It is common for students to assume that they have mastered a piece of music, only to discover, to their disappointment, that when tested in performance, their results fall short of their expectations. They often erroneously believe that if they have managed to play a piece a few times with "only a small number of mistakes," they should then be able to perform the piece proficiently for a lesson or even in front of an audience. The result can be extremely disheartening and embarrassing. To explain their poor performances, students will often say things such as "It was far better at home" (or "in the practice room") or "I had no problem with it last night." Their sense of bewilderment can often lead to discouragement, since their own musical judgment and ability have been brought into question. They often believe that they have acquired the confidence to perform proficiently, only to discover that their confidence was premature.

HOW I LEARNED TO SHIFT WITH MY LEFT ARM
WHILE DRIVING THROUGH THE
BRITISH COUNTRYSIDE
1. Beginning: London

If it is to be confidently and solidly learned, a skill will go through several stages. To demonstrate the way in which students develop skills at the piano, I offer a personal anecdote that involves learning a physical activity.

A few years ago, my family and I took our annual vacation in Great Britain. In the belief that I was a competent driver, I decided to rent a car, and driving with a stick shift on the "wrong" side of the road seemed like a fun challenge at the time. When my family and I arrived at the London rental agency, I was reminded of one important detail that I had forgotten when planning the trip: not only was I going to have to drive on the left side of the road, but I was also going to have to shift with my left arm. This turned a fine challenge into an abject nightmare, since I had no kinesthetic memory at all for driving a stick shift with my left arm. I was going to have to learn from scratch while fighting midtown traffic in London on the way to the highway.

After a rather bumpy start, we cautiously made our way through the maze of London city streets, hoping to get to the outskirts of London and finally onto the A1 highway. My kids were instructed to remind me frequently to keep to the left, while I had the task of talking to my left arm: "OK, first gear is up and to the left, watch out for that taxi." (My son: "Keep left, Dad.") "OK, time for second gear; clutch; second gear is down and to the left. Hey! This is not so bad. Oh, no, just stalled out in the middle of the intersection." (My daughter: "Keep left, Dad.") "Making a right turn is complicated; one must remember to look both ways. OK, first gear left and up." (My wife: "*Keep left!*") "Clutch, second gear left and down, getting ready for third gear. Oh, no! Shifted by mistake into fifth, which is all the way over to the right and up. I need the one in the middle [expletive deleted]! Stalled out . . ." Nevertheless, after experiencing more excitement than we bargained for, somehow we made it out of London and onto the A1 highway.

2. Making Progress: On the A1

During the next third of the journey, while we were driving mainly on highways and just before getting to Wales, I had sufficiently mastered certain intricacies of shifting to allow us to listen to a few chapters of the *Harry Potter* recording we had brought along for the journey. But alas, just as we were about to enter Wales, we had to curtail our listening, to my children's great disappointment. While certain aspects of shifting had become internalized, I was forced to turn off *Harry Potter* so that I could return to my conversation with my left arm. Why? Because of the numerous roundabouts that I now had to carefully negotiate. And in Britain, roundabouts go "backward," that is, clockwise, in contrast to the counterclockwise direction that I was used to in the United States. "Clutch, neutral, first or second gear; no, the one down to the left. Oh, got it. Whew! Didn't stall."

3. Smooth Arrival

Subsequent roundabouts went better, and by the sixth one, I hardly had to think about most of the procedure, but still, as my daughter helpfully pointed out, I was driving like my grandmother. Things improved markedly during the last tenth of the trip, when I was able to drive, talk to my family, *and* listen to *Harry Potter* without stalling once. Finally, after a full day on the road, during which my driving progressed from extremely halting to almost instinctive, we arrived at our destination.

BECOMING AN EXPERT

The manner in which I had acquired my left-arm acumen with the gear-shift can be contextualized in the three learning stages that are required to gain expertise in any skill.

Anders Ericsson, one of the foremost authorities in the field of skill acquisition, describes expertise as follows:

> Expertise refers to the mechanisms underlying the superior achievement of an expert, i.e. one who has acquired special skill in or knowledge of a particular subject through professional training and practical experience. The term expert . . . includes any individual who attained their superior performance by instruction and extended practice. (Ericsson 2000)

Experts display such comprehensive, natural, and seemingly effortless ability that a casual observer may mistake it for natural, inborn ability. What may generally not be understood is the fact that the expert has spent enormous amounts of time in acquiring expertise. It is reasonable to assume, based on Ericsson's research, that the greater the time spent in practice, the better the result. This fact has recently been highlighted by Malcolm Gladwell in his book *Outliers: The Story of Success* (2008), in which he emphasizes the importance of enormous numbers of hours of practice in order to reach the level of an expert. He states that top performers manage to practice approximately one thousand hours per year and that true expertise occurs only after ten years of such practicing.

FITTS AND POSNER'S PHASES OF LEARNING

In 1967, in what has become an acknowledged classic model of learning stages, researchers Paul M. Fitts and Michael I. Posner described three steps that an individual passes through on the way to acquiring a skill. One of the first studies of its kind, Fitts and Posner's original research was to become decisive in the then-new area of skill acquisition. Their model continues to this day to be cited by motor-learning specialists whose main concern is how we attain skill in performing a given action.

This elegant model, to be called "phases of learning" by Posner, provides three easy-to-understand steps that may easily be applied to practicing the piano. As we will see, they perfectly parallel the learning stages I experienced while driving through England and Wales. There are three phases, but the transitions between them are gradual and somewhat indistinct. I am sure that when you finish reading this section, you, too, will be able to think of many times you traversed these stages on the way to learning a new skill, whether it was tying your shoes, riding a bike, or even preparing a favorite recipe. As learning progresses, one phase merges gradually into the next, so that no definite transition between them is apparent.

The Cognitive Stage

As depicted in figure 3.1, the first of the three stages is the cognitive stage, in which the individual thinks about the skill that he or she is about to learn. In this phase, the individual in most skill-acquisition situations tries to understand the task and what it demands. That is what took place at the outset of my journey, when I began "telling" my left arm where all the gears were and how to get to them. Improvement is rapid, but movements can be jerky and uncoordinated (my family, to this day, can attest to this fact). High levels of concentration (there was silence in the car, no *Harry Potter* yet) and attention are needed during this stage. Thus, a considerable amount of internal self-talk or self-direction takes place. One generally verbalizes questions such as "What is my objective?" or "How far should I move my arm?"

Figure 3.1 Fitts and Posner's three stages of learning

The Associative Stage

During the associative stage, the intermediate phase of skill acquisition, patterns that have been learned as individual units during the early phase of skill learning are ironed out as new secure patterns of learning begin to emerge. Errors, which can be frequent at first, are gradually eliminated. In this stage, single chunks are joined and become bigger chunks. The learner shows a great deal more consistency, and coordination improves much more rapidly. As a newcomer to the British form of driving, I began to enter this phase as we left the densely trafficked areas of midtown London and began to head toward the outskirts and onto the highway (we were also able to restart *Harry Potter*). During this phase, one refines one's attempts, and consistency begins to increase. Improvements in timing and rhythm also occur. At this point, the basic mechanics of the skill are present. There is also increasingly less cognitive mediation or self-talk.

The Autonomous Stage

The last stage of learning is called the autonomous stage. At this stage, one is capable of producing skilled actions automatically, with little or no conscious control over the movements being executed. Movements become increasingly independent, less directly subject to cognitive control, and less subject to interference from other ongoing activities or environmental distractions. In this phase, skills require less mental processing. Movements are smoother and more efficient, because less mental intervention is needed to carry out the skill. There is little conscious control of one's movements as the action becomes flowing. In addition, distractions that may previously have had an impact on the performance now have little or no effect. This is what I experienced when, at long last, I reached our destination in Wales with a well-educated and autonomous left arm. These stages of learning, as demonstrated by my experiences in learning to drive in Britain, are applicable to the development of any skill and, for the purposes of this book, will be applied to the piano and to achieving flow.

PHASES OF LEARNING APPLIED TO PIANO PRACTICE

Since most piano students are not expecting to reach the lofty level of expert in the immediate future, it is necessary to determine how they should assess progress to the point of solid attainment. Put another way, how does a student recognize when a piece of music has been worked on to the point that it has been mastered to the extent that it can be confidently performed in public? Or how do students know when they have really learned a piece of music?

The following description of the three learning stages as delineated by Fitts and Posner will aid you, the pianist, in assessing your place along the phases of learning continuum (see figure 3.1).

Cognitive

When playing the piano, you may ask such questions as "What are these notes?" "At what angle should I place my hand?" "How do I interpret this rhythm?" and "What is the best finger to use on the F-sharp?" A possible example of verbalization is to say the names of the notes or harmonies aloud as you practice. An additional subject of the internal dialogue taking place could be related to finding the perfect gesture to fit a given task. Your laborious decoding of the score, deliberate checking of fingering, or writing in accidentals indicates that you are in the cognitive stage. Because of the intensity of the self-talk, many gross errors are committed in executing the actions, which can lead to inconsistency and moment-to-moment variability in performances (resulting in stalling out or frequent wrong notes).

Associative

The associative stage, the major stage of practicing, is the one in which you will gradually pick up tempo and no longer have to expend mental resources in decoding the score (reciting the names of the notes aloud has by now become a thing of the past). At the low associative stage, you may observe that much of the excerpt still requires the self-talk common in the cognitive phase, whereas in the high associative phase, it is just the opposite: little self-talk or direction giving and a great amount of fluidity. In the mid-associative range, fluidity and self-talk will be approximately equal.

In this stage, the single steps of the excerpt are chunked together (more about this later), and through repetition, performance becomes proceduralized. You make fewer errors, since through repetition (often "massive," implying very many iterations), you gradually attain the task's basic movements. Also, during this stage, you refine your movement. Notes and rhythmic accuracy improve and are accompanied by a growing expressivity and increased tempo. It becomes less necessary to think of the action of the hands, as muscle memory begins to emerge, resulting in your being able to play more and more of the excerpt without conscious thought. Csikszentmihalyi observes that the "flow experience is typically described as involving a sense of control—or more precisely, as lacking the sense of worry about losing control."

Autonomous

You should now be able to play your excerpt or piece of music with ever-increasing efficiency, accuracy, expressivity, and speed. You will note that the excerpt you are working on begins to flow, and your physical movement has become more efficient and perhaps even graceful. In addition, distractions that may previously have had an impact on the performance no longer have a significant effect. You are able to perform the passage consistently well from one attempt to another. Csikszentmihalyi identifies this stage of autonomy as one in which the "sense of control of one's activities emerges as an important criterion for the flow experience" (1990, 134). Completion of this step will enable you to perform at an artistic level in which your own individual interpretation and ideas come to the fore.

DEFINING TASKS AND LEARNING STRATEGIES: CHUNKING

Learning through recognition and implementation of patterns can be accomplished by breaking a task into a collection of "chunks" and then combining the chunks that have been learned into a single task. The proper organization, sequencing, and repetition of several clusters gradually become united into a larger chunk and eventually into a unified whole, just as I learned the various sequential movements involved in shifting (first gear moving seamlessly to second gear, and so on) as a series of separate motions as I drove through England. The familiar process by which advanced pianists learn scales and arpeggios is an obvious form of chunking, so that certain frequently occurring patterns can be easily recognized and executed when they are encountered in the repertory.

In now-famous experiments involving chess players, researchers William G. Chase and Herbert A. Simon (Gobet et al. 2001) further illustrated the

importance of chunking. They compared chess masters to novices and ana-
lyzed both groups' abilities to memorize varying game-board positions.
They discovered that the chess masters had enormous powers of recall and
were able to reconstruct any board configuration with great accuracy after
the pieces were removed from the board. The novices were able to replace
only a handful of pieces. However, when the pieces were assembled on the
chessboard at random, helter-skelter, with the pieces occupying squares in
a way that bore no resemblance to a real game, amazingly, both novices and
masters performed at about the same level. What became apparent from
this experiment was that the chess masters had memorized real game situations as chunks, just as we see a jumble of letters and recognize a word.

As we shall see in chapter 4, chunking while practicing the piano is
essential to learning and enjoyment. However, most pianists seldom do
this, instead approaching learning a new piece of music without an organizational plan. The following excerpt from the beginning of a Telemann
minuet provides an example of how one may divide a piece of music into
chunks of varying size:

The first right-hand unit may consist of:

The next unit would then be:

Mastery of both right-hand chunks together would then follow:

The first left-hand unit may consist of:

And it would be followed by:

Mastery of both of these left-hand units would then take place:

Intermediate matching of left- and right-hand chunks together could look like this:

Putting these chunks together would culminate in the unified whole:

SELF-DOUBT AND THE CORROSIVE
POWER OF *SHOULD*

Nothing will more surely lead you to unwise decisions when you are choosing what to practice than the double-edged sword of self-doubt and the awful word *should*. Self-doubt's debilitating effects can permeate your entire being, affecting both your mental and physical states and ultimately short-circuiting all attempts at improvement. Timothy Gallwey, author of *The Inner Game of Golf*, believes that doubt is most likely the fundamental cause of error. He states that doubts "have a tendency to become self-fulfilling prophecies" and that when "doubt is directed toward one's potential to learn and to perform or toward one's very self, it can be quite detrimental. . . . The primary gap that exists between what a person is *capable* of doing and experiencing and what he or she actually *does* do and experience" (Gallwey 2009, 49).

All musicians suffer from debilitating thoughts of doubt and negative self-criticism from time to time. It is widely recognized that such negative thinking is counterproductive and frequently leads to deep feelings of inadequacy. The crux of the problem can be summarized in a single word: *should*. The list of "I should *this*" and "I should *that*" goes on and on. Take your pick. Surely, at some time, you have uttered mentally (or perhaps even out loud) one of these negative statements:

- What's wrong with me? I keep making the same error(s). I *should* be able to play this easily.
- What's wrong with me? Lenny plays it so well, and I'm just as good as, if not better than, he is. I *should* be able to do this.
- What's wrong with me? I've been studying now for ten years. After so much time, I *should* be at a more advanced place.

Tragically, this can lead to the following sorts of attitude:

- I'm really not very good at this.
- Why has the piano become so joyless?
- Maybe I'll take a break from lessons.

To be fair, inquiring into what *should* be can lead one to make an honest assessment of oneself, but too often, it leads to despondency, depression, and a negative self-regard. Life is too short for such an outlook. And such an outlook slows down the learning process considerably or even brings it to a grinding halt. If we question the use of the word *should*, we might discover that there is no "one size fits all" evaluation mechanism when it comes to playing the piano and that we all travel on different paths in our lives. Such a point of view, often associated with Eastern philosophical approaches, may help somewhat, yet it can't provide the full solution to the nagging feeling that something needs to improve.

RADICAL ACCEPTANCE AT THE PIANO

Radical acceptance is the practice of accepting life's givens, or in the words of Reinhold Niebuhr's serenity prayer, to accept the things you cannot change. Tara Brach, clinical psychologist and author of *Radical Acceptance: Embracing Your Life with the Heart of a Buddha* (2004), found that many of her clients were burdened by a sense of unworthiness. This feeling too often inhabits the minds of those studying the piano. The antidote to this is *radical acceptance*, which can enable you to see yourself with greater clarity. It means not being passive but accepting "what is" with the understanding that you have the power of choice. Practicing radical acceptance is a choice that can help you avoid feelings of unworthiness and the stress that can accompany piano practice. Paradoxically, according to this approach to life, change can happen only when you unequivocally accept your current state of being.

Knowing your strengths and abilities in order to take on appropriate challenges is therefore an important prerequisite to change. Here are a few commands worth internalizing:

1. *Be gentle with yourself.* This will mean something different for each of us. Basically, ask whether you are being too tough on yourself with your moment-to-moment expectations. Even if the answer is "I don't know" or "Maybe," ease off. It is better to err on the side of gentleness.
2. *Praise yourself.* Every time something goes as well as or even better than expected, tell yourself how well you are doing, and stop criticizing yourself.
3. *Accept yourself.* Don't listen to the little voice inside you that says you aren't good enough to learn. You simply have to find the right practice strategy.

In order to do the above and get on the road to radical acceptance, it will be necessary to rid yourself of all the *shoulds* you may have come to accept. In order to see yourself with the necessary clarity, it will be helpful to judge your progress on any particular fragment, phrase, section, or entire piece on which you are working according to the phases of learning continuum that I have provided (and on which I will expand further in chapter 4). Familiarity with these steps can help you to recognize approximately how far your efforts have taken you on the road to mastery.

Fitts and Posner suggested that feedback provides information that can be processed to add to your understanding of the skill, task, or activity being studied and indicate how close you are to achieving a given goal. Having this information at your disposal can yield significant benefits, since it will enable you to have an objective sense of what portion of the skill has been learned and what remains to be accomplished. This may mean, for instance, that of the eight measures of a particular phrase, you may have already mastered or reached the autonomous stage in six of them. Therefore, your current responsibility is reduced to only the two remaining measures. Avoid such statements as "I should be able to play all eight measures" or "I'm not sure I'll ever be able to play these measures flawlessly." Simply focus on those two measures, even if they initially have to be broken down into smaller units of perhaps only half a measure long. Once those two measures have also been brought to the autonomous stage, you can then work on all eight measures as a unit. Such information can act as an indicator or even as a reward, which can motivate you to continue working. This motivation is an important, perhaps even necessary, condition for learning.

CHAPTER 4

Combining Flow and Skills

In this chapter, we explore how the three phases of learning flow together so that every practice session yields solid results. We formulate methods to use our own emotional responses to tell us how to proceed. For the time being, it is important to understand that elite musicians, dancers, athletes, and experts in all fields have achieved mastery not simply through hard work but also through smart practicing. The chapter provides insights into how any pianist can do the same no matter where he or she is on the continuum of mastery.

Before exploring these essential ingredients for learning, we touch on a most important topic. As all students of piano realize, with the exception of the one hour a week spent with a teacher, all learning must be done on your own. There will be no one present in the room while you are practicing except yourself, your thoughts, and your attentiveness. In other words, during these hours, you will be in charge of your own learning. This is vitally important, for the successful directing of your learning will point you, like a well-shot arrow, directly to your goal. However, trying to become your own teacher during these lonely hours can be a formidable undertaking. The question is, therefore, how do we direct our own learning and become excellent self-teachers and learners?

SELF-TEACHING

Studies of self-regulation have shown that people who are successful are skilled at creating an engine for continuous learning. They have mastered the following steps, which we will hereinafter refer to as Power Steps for Learning (PSLs):

1. They know how to choose learning goals.
2. They reflect on learning strategies.
3. They are conscious of how to sustain motivation.

Those who are less adept at self-teaching often have difficulty at first in focusing on a particular set of goals. Without a focus, it is difficult to come up with learning strategies, and the result is poorly directed practice, leading to little progress and eventual loss of motivation. All pianists have contended with these issues, for the oceans of possibility that confront us as we scan a new piece of music for some sign of entry can be overwhelming. Where and how to begin are among the most daunting tasks with which all artists, no matter what their domain, have to contend.

Once we have focused on how to begin, we now have to decide on a set of learning strategies and, perhaps as important, learn to recognize when learning is taking place. Am I spinning my wheels? Am I going in the right direction? Perhaps I'll just put on the metronome and ramp it up bit by bit—surely, learning is taking place if I can play it faster. All these doubts have plagued the best of us from time to time, yet we may persevere, since, after all, we are at the altar of music, and isn't suffering a noble path to learning? Shouldn't I be gratified at the perceived progress I gain through pain? Society tells me over and over, "No pain, no gain." Perhaps there is a reward later on in life, or maybe it is in the afterlife that I will finally be content.

No! No! No! This spinning of wheels is decidedly antithetical to learning, since this way of directing our learning is discouraging and joyless. Ultimately, how can we excel and rise to the heights of artistry if our lot is to suffer daily?

ACHIEVING THE ULTIMATE STATE FOR LEARNING

Human beings are naturally inquisitive. If you have ever watched a young child exploring the same toy over and over, you will surely agree that it is in our nature to want to learn. However, pianists often engage in moment-to-moment study techniques that do not fuel a desire to continue to learn. In order to sustain motivation, we need to be willing to work and to feel that our efforts are paying off with positive results. A successful and willing learner is one who is able to consistently utilize the three PSLs of deciding what to learn, determining appropriate learning techniques or strategies, and doing so in a way that fuels their own motivation to continue. The approach of *success + volition* is thus far superior to the approach that accepts practicing as drudgery that must be undertaken to achieve the golden result of musical mastery and doesn't recognize that those moment-to-moment decisions may reduce motivation. Yet *success + volition*, or being successful at a process that we do willingly, still is insufficient to produce optimal results.

Think of individuals you know who seem to possess endless energy and joy in their life and their profession. The late Steve Jobs, of Apple fame, comes to mind. Yet history is replete with such extraordinary individuals whose productivity and consistent genius seem to defy all human limitations. How, we ask, can one man create such an abundance of magnificent art? And yet there have been giants such as, Renoir, Picasso, Degas, Titian, Michelangelo, Shakespeare, Bach, Mozart, Beethoven, Brahms, Bartók, Stravinsky, Verdi. and countless other geniuses in all the arts and throughout the ages who seemed to defy the limitations imposed by time and the human condition. Magnificent scientists, philosophers, and scholarly geniuses also fall into this staggeringly great category.

The great pianists such as Liszt, Leschetizky, Horowitz, Arrau, Rubinstein, and many others spent countless hours honing their craft. How did they do it? What was the source of their endless energy? Just as these giants of pianism did, in order to rise to your maximal capability to learn and create, you must sincerely enjoy the experience of learning. It is a fundamental error to believe that enjoyment is something to be wished for in some idealized future but never attained in the present. In fact, recent research maintains unequivocally that all of us have an underlying desire and ability to be joyful in learning, especially in pursuits that add value to our existence. My own research has shown that my piano students who made moment-to-moment learning decisions based on an explicit goal of achieving flow, in which enjoyment is maximal, made far greater progress than those who shared the goal of learning repertoire but pursued that goal in a manner that gave little value to the enjoyment of the learning process. The "happy" students in my study made gains that were objectively superior to those of the students who attempted to "grin and bear it." The highest state of learning, therefore, may be summed up as *success + volition + enjoyment*. In other words, if our efforts consistently yield results, our desire to learn will increase greatly. This is particularly true if our efforts are also enjoyable. And that leads to success, to greater enjoyment, and on to greater success.

Nevertheless, having the requisite organizational tools to make possible the first part of the equation—success—depends on the three PSLs of (1) focusing on the right material for learning, (2) knowing the steps to take to ensure learning, and (3) fueling one's motivation for learning through the successful implementation of steps 1 and 2.

LEARNING AND FLOW

Both phases of learning and flow experience involve engagement in an activity for the purpose of enhanced and effective learning. As we will see, if applied together, they can provide the foundation necessary to encourage optimal learning by leading the individual to the PSLs.

Those who experience flow while engaging in a challenging activity, such as learning a new dance step or a new way of putting topspin on a tennis serve, will invariably pass through the three phases of learning as described by Fitts and Posner. When flow is present, then, as one passes through the phases of learning on one's way to becoming an expert, time will seem to fly, concentration will be total, action and awareness will merge, and the activity will become enjoyable in and of itself. It is also important to note that as one becomes better and better at executing a task, an increase in overall self-esteem and confidence should also take place. All of these are characteristics associated with flow.

Flow can occur during any of the three phases of learning—cognitive, associative, and autonomous—and moreover, it is most likely to occur when there is a balance between perceived challenges and perceived skills. As we discuss below, flow is least likely to emerge during the cognitive stage of learning.

The following is a summary of each phase of learning and how flow may drive and enhance the learning experience.

Flow in the Cognitive Phase

This stage is the one in which the greatest amount of "internal dialogue" takes place, as the pianist attempts to find the gesture that is a perfect fit for the given musical task. As has already been stated, there is usually a twenty-minute start-up before flow has the opportunity to emerge. If one has chosen one's challenge carefully enough and not attempted to learn anything too complex, then the cognitive stage is the stage that often takes the least time to complete. That is why flow is not likely to emerge during the cognitive stage of learning.

Flow characteristics during this phase:

- Clear goals and immediate feedback should drive and be present in this phase. If these characteristics are not present, then the excerpt being practiced is either inappropriate in its entirety or requires simplification.
- Complete involvement, clear goals, and immediate feedback in an activity are key to the creation of an optimal learning experience.

Probability of flow emerging during this phase: Low.

Flow in the Associative Phase

In this stage, single steps are chunked together and through repetition become proceduralized. The student makes fewer errors, since through repetition he attains the task's basic movements. In addition, during this stage, the performer refines his attempts, resulting in increased reliability. There is also gradually less verbalization of the process, associated with an increasing ability to perform certain aspects of the action without conscious thought.

Flow characteristics during this phase:

- Greatly enhanced concentration and focus begin to emerge.
- The sense of worry associated with losing control gradually disappears.
- Awareness increasingly merges with action.

Probability of flow emerging during this phase:

- Low at the early associative stage.
- Moderate at the mid-associative stage.
- Moderate to great at the high associative stage.

Flow in the Autonomous Phase

The performer is able to play the given excerpt or piece of music with ever-increasing tempo efficiency, accuracy, and expressivity. Cognitive mediation is at a minimum, and there is little conscious control of movement, which has become automatic, more efficient, and even graceful, as the music begins to flow. In addition, distractions that may previously have had an impact on the performance no longer have a significant effect.

The student is able to perform the passage consistently well from one attempt to another.

Flow characteristics during this phase:

- Full concentration begins to emerge.
- Self-consciousness and irrelevant thinking disappear.
- Awareness and action are fully merged.

Probability of flow emerging during this phase: Great.

BEST MINDSET FOR INTEGRATING FLOW AND SKILL BUILDING

Learning a piece of music can be a very complicated affair, in that the challenges that one encounters can vary greatly from moment to moment. Every phrase will have numerous challenges that need to be addressed and mastered. Identifying and breaking these challenges down into chunks of musical segments and mastering these one by one can reap excellent results. In chapter 3, we saw how a line of a Telemann minuet could be approached systematically. Using this step-by-step approach to learning repertoire, however, is effective only if the pianist is motivated to do so in a manner that maintains interest and has the potential of leading to mastery.

If we approach learning a segment of music in a lackadaisical, unfocused, and unenthusiastic manner ("LAX"), we will most likely become inattentive to the detail contained in the segment as our minds wander to other subjects. This approach is completely antithetical to flow, in that mindless inattention to detail suppresses the occurrence of the important flow characteristic of full control. When our imaginations are not fully engaged, part of our consciousness is left out of the equation. This is the opposite of the important flow characteristic that action and awareness become one.

The opposite of a lackadaisical approach, the "Type A" overzealous ("TAOZ") mode of working, is equally problematic. Those of TAOZ type are often praised as go-getters and thought of as being highly responsible as they brush aside all obstacles in pursuit of perfection. Such people are often complimented on their hard work and held up as paragons of virtue. However, it is also well known that TAOZ types often suffer a variety of ailments as a result of their excessive zeal. In 1950, medical researchers Meyer Friedman and Ray Rosenman determined that Type A behavior doubles the risk of coronary heart disease in otherwise healthy individuals. In addition to its obvious negative implications for health and based on my own research and experience, a TAOZ approach to learning music often leads one to attempt to learn music that is of a complexity that is far above one's ability. In this scenario, the individual rides roughshod over all the segment's complications and works under the harmful principle of "no pain, no gain." The TAOZ type readily admits that the process is painful and asserts that martyrdom at the altar of music is worth the sacrifice of attempting to learn a segment of music that is really too difficult. This is not a terribly uplifting approach to creating art. Nor will it foster repeat performances. For who truly wishes to suffer for their art—especially on a continual daily basis?

CHOOSING THE CHALLENGE

The TAOZ individual will gladly suffer frustration, while the LAX individual will willingly tolerate the opposite, which is boredom. For the former, the challenge is too far above the ability of the individual, while for the latter, the opposite is true: the individual's skill is well above the chosen challenge. Both of these situations are decidedly antithetical to flow, in that the primary criterion for flow to emerge is that challenge needs to be well matched or only slightly above one's perceived ability. This is as close to a cardinal rule as there is in setting up a flow-inducing activity. Figure 4.1 depicts this balance.

The interaction of flow and phases of learning within a given segment is a dynamic process, that is, an activity that is continuous and productive. As depicted in figure 4.2, flow can occur during any of the three phases of learning—cognitive, associative, and autonomous—and moreover, it is most likely to occur when there is a "balance between perceived challenges

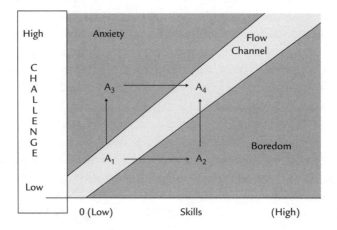

Figure 4.1 The flow channel

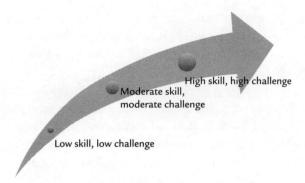

Figure 4.2 The relationship between flow and levels of skill and challenge

and perceived skills" (Abuhamdeh, Csikszentmihalyi, and Nakamura 2005) and particularly at the higher levels of skill and challenge.

Of course—and you may have already figured this out—small segments of music can be mastered rather quickly. In fact, the whole process of learning a small segment can often be accomplished in a few minutes. Because of the relatively short amount of time spent learning a simple segment, it is unlikely that flow can emerge (recall that at least twenty to twenty-five minutes of mindful practice usually must take place before flow has a chance of occurring). However, in order to keep challenge and skill constantly in balance, it is essential that the mastery of simple segments leads to the linking of those segments into passages of greater complexity and length. Because of the increased time needed to master a longer segment, it is during this period—when the pianist spends increasingly greater amounts of time on segments of greater complexity—that flow has the greatest chance of emerging.

The emergence of flow depends on several ingredients, divided into two segments of the practice session:

Setup: first twenty to twenty-five minutes
1. *The successful choice of segments in which the challenge is well matched to the perception of one's skill level at the time.* Usually, it is best to choose a segment that is slightly above the perceived skill level (never below, since that could lead to boredom).
2. *The mastery of these simple segments during the initial stages of practice so they have an optimal chance of being chunked or linked.*

Flow: the rest of the session
3. *The chunking or linking of these longer segments into larger, more complex segments that require greater and greater amounts of time on*

task. Again, it is important that the challenge created by combining the smaller segments be at or slightly above the pianist's perceived skill level. As time on task increases, so does the possibility that flow may emerge.

Times like these, in which one makes positive gains in an enjoyable fashion, are to be cherished. Being in flow becomes its own reward, which then creates a desire to duplicate that experience. The desire to enter a long, sustained period of flow thus fuels the initial efforts, whose complexity may be insufficient to sustain a long period of flow or even the possibility of its emergence.

Figures 4.3, 4.4, 4.5, and 4.6 show that mastery increases as the need for planning and internal dialogue diminishes. They also show that as this process takes place and as one progresses through the learning stages, the possibility that flow may emerge increases. The diminishment of planning and internal dialogue and the rise of mastery when internal dialogue has all but disappeared are also illustrated.

Figure 4.7 suggests the complex process by which careful segmentation of a piece of music, practice, and the ongoing assessment of the balance between challenge and skill level, flow, and the current phase of learning interact as the student works toward mastery. For example, since flow is likely to occur when skill level and challenge are well matched, the presence or absence of flow can be used as an indicator of whether one has assumed a challenge that is too difficult, too easy, or commensurate with one's skill level. If the challenge is too great, the student should move to a simpler segment or perhaps subdivide the current segment into smaller, more digestible pieces. If the student's skill level is beyond the level of the challenge, the student should continue practice until mastery of the segment is achieved at the autonomous phase of learning.

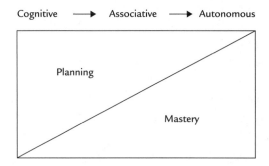

Figure 4.3 As one progresses through practice stages, planning the action diminishes as mastery increases

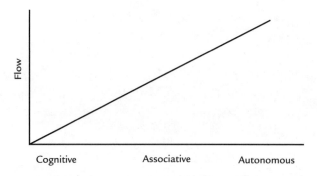

Figure 4.4 The possibility of flow increases as one progresses through these stages

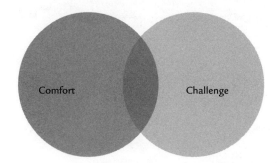

Figure 4.5 An overlapping space exists where one is comfortable with the challenges presented, and flow is most likely to occur in that space

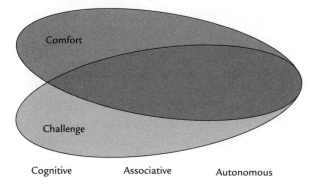

Figure 4.6 The space that overlaps—where flow is possible—increases as one progresses through learning stages

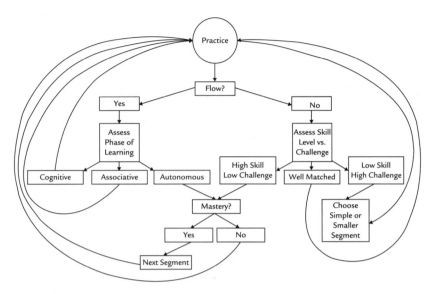

Figure 4.7 The practice flow chart: Continual assessment of flow and phase of learning guides the student's practice

SUMMARY

Recall that the three steps to self-regulated learning, the PSLs, involve focusing on the segment to be learned, choosing and implementing effective learning steps, and executing these steps in a manner that provides further incentive to continue. These three steps constitute the first twenty to twenty-five minutes of learning (the first part of the setup). I advocate that this first step, before flow has had the opportunity to emerge, must be gentle, with a self-conscious attempt to create conditions whereby motivation to continue learning is built in. The steps of choosing what and how to practice figure greatly in one's desire to continue and to reap the benefits that accrue when flow emerges. So the best way to implement a beginning plan for practicing is to carefully choose a chunk for learning in which the steps to accomplishment are clear (recall that clarity of goal is a characteristic of flow) and have the potential of providing maximal motivation for further learning. In addition, to provide flow potential, the chunk should be slightly above one's perceived level of skill. In chapter 5, we examine a simple piece of music and suggest a learning procedure that takes into consideration all the concepts covered so far: self-regulatory issues, the three PSLs, phases of learning, and flow.

Learning a Simple Piece

Flow can emerge only when certain conditions are present. Principally, the challenge that you select must be perceived to be only slightly above your skill level. In addition, throughout the process, it is essential to monitor your reactions to make sure that the emotions of frustration, anxiety, boredom, and apathy are not present. Therefore, when you are practicing, you must learn to trust your own feelings regarding your own reactions to what you are doing. Again, this may be hard for some of us, since we are programmed to disregard our feelings and just trudge along, tolerating negative emotions as a price to be paid for success. But such acceptance of negative emotions must be overcome if we are to make it possible for flow to emerge.

PREPARING TO GO INTO FLOW

What follows is an example of a procedure designed to create flow-enhancing conditions. This plan will be guided by the "phases of learning" model, leading you on your way to mastery. Following this plan carefully will enable both flow and mastery to emerge together.

It is extremely important not to assume that you must learn this piece in order from beginning to end. It is important that you choose practicing segments for their potential to provide an adequate challenge, one that is neither too difficult nor too easy. For some, that may mean starting somewhere in the middle, while others may decide to begin elsewhere. Let us review the three phases of learning through the following excerpt of an easy piano piece by Beethoven:

German Dance

Ludwig van Beethoven (1770-1827)

COGNITIVE PHASE

The first goal-oriented attempts at performing a skill involve thinking about the skill as much as executing it.

The first stage of learning this piece of music involves learning the notes. For this, you must obviously first observe that the piece is in the key of A major. In addition to knowing where the notes are on the keyboard, you must also learn the rhythm and be responsive to expressive indications. In this stage of learning, you should be as consumed with decoding the notes as you are with playing them.

Implications

a. Poor rhythmical flow and coordination.

Because of your unfamiliarity with the music, you are unlikely to perform in a manner that is fluid and coordinated.

b. Simple, clear introduction to skill.

In this phase of learning, you must decide on the best procedure for learning the piece.

c. Focusing on one or two aspects of the skill at a time.

You must now choose the size and nature of the challenge of the "learning unit" so that it is just slightly above your current skill level. Some possible choices of learning units are as follows:

A. Right hand

B. Right hand

C. Left hand

D. Left hand

E. Right hand

F. Right hand

G. Left hand

H. Left hand

For the more skilled pianist:

I. Right hand

J. Left hand

K. Right hand

L. Left hand

For the most skilled:

M. Both hands

N. Both hands

d. Responding to feedback and making adjustments.

After choosing the level of challenge that you believe to be only slightly above your current level of skill, you should begin mastery of only one of your chosen learning units. It is essential to keep in mind that flow can exist only if the goals are clear and there is an appropriate match between skill and challenge. Thus, trying to learn more than one unit at a time will lead to confusion, since the goals of each will be different. Your feedback will be derived from the ability to play the chosen segment in a manner that is technically accurate and musically expressive.

Since another goal is to be so immersed in the activity that normal concerns disappear, the conditions must be ideal for the merging of action and awareness and the emergence of deliberate gesture. Attempting to accomplish something far beyond your capability or to accomplish too much at once will be flow-inhibiting.

e. Gradually increased emphasis on form.

You should now deliberately focus on the quality of the gesture related to the practice portion that has been chosen. If, for instance, you have selected the following,

D. Left hand

it may be played staccato, for instance, with a deliberate gesture that flexes the fingernail joint flexor tendons. You will observe that the resulting bounce feels right and achieves the desired sound at a slow but easily manageable tempo. If you are practicing

E. Right hand

you may choose to focus on the phrase-ending lift at the end of each measure, making sure that this gesture adequately sets up the position for beginning the next phrase fluently.

ASSOCIATIVE PHASE

Through frequent repetition of the practice portion, you gradually begin to organize your kinesthetic processes so that the desired sound emerges in the most efficient manner possible. If you are practicing

A. Right hand

you will have already eliminated mistakes involving pitch and rhythmic accuracy in the cognitive stage. Possible difficulties may arise as a result of the change of hand position that occurs between the first and second measures. In order to solve this, you may wish to work on the release gesture of the last note of measure 1 and the arrival of the thumb on measure 2. Subsequent to this, it may be useful to repeat the second measure until the five notes are played fluently.

Implications

a. Improved synchronization of temporal and spatial elements of movement. The tempo at which you can play the unit increases as a result of the ever-diminishing size of the staccato releases and the efficiency and size of the move from the first to the second measure. Expression also steadily improves. The repeated notes are distinctly different from the legato notes in terms of articulation and tone. The five notes of the second measure are performed increasingly with a slight crescendo into the third note that is followed by a slight diminuendo.
b. Greater control and rhythmical coordination.
As you combine the two efforts outlined above, the passage gradually becomes more fluent, the tempo increases, and with increased technical control, you now should begin to play with ever-increasing expressivity. The three staccato bounces of the third finger in the first measure now lead to the legato of the second measure. A causal relationship between the first and second measures thus emerges.

As gross errors disappear, control will increase, and action and awareness will begin to merge. Freed from the distraction of wrong notes, you should gradually become more invested in the activity. Thus, flow now has a greater chance of emerging if it hasn't occurred already. The self-correcting behavior of the cognitive phase has now led to gestures that are increasingly deliberate and sure.

AUTONOMOUS PHASE

The skill has become habitual, performance variability and accompanying worrying thoughts concerning errors has diminished greatly. The passage has become automatic, and any small errors that may occur can be corrected without a great expenditure of energy or focus.

Implications

Practice should enhance form, style, and accuracy. In this stage of development, you perform the excerpt with efficiency, accuracy, and speed, with little need of conscious control over the technical aspects of the music. The main concern is with expressive elements such as dynamics, tone production, articulation, character, and tempo. You no longer must think about the individual notes, for they have become second nature. Instead, you may concentrate on one or two difficult aspects, such as the leap between measures 1 and 2 and imparting greater musical meaning through control of tone, volume, and articulation.

A perfect blend between skill and challenge has occurred. You should now be so fully immersed in the excerpt that it can be played with expressive freedom. There is a total merging of action and awareness. Time ceases to be a factor, and the goal, which is to play as beautifully as possible, is utterly clear and attainable by a gesture that is deliberate and sure. All these factors lead to enhanced self-esteem and lack of self-consciousness, which should motivate an application of this procedure to the remaining learning units.

PUTTING THE PIECES TOGETHER

The preceding description of how one might learn a piece of music modeled after Fitts and Posner's "phases of learning" and relating it to Csikszentmihalyi's flow attributes pertains to the learning of practice portions that may be quite small (examples A, C, and D). In order for this section of the piece to be learned in its entirety, these smaller pieces may need to be put together both horizontally, as in learning the entire section with hands separate, and vertically, as in learning a unit with hands together. Utilizing the "phases of learning" principles with flow as outlined above and after learning practice portions A through H one at a time, you might want to combine portions in the following order:

A and B. Right hand

C and D. Left hand

A and C. Hands together

B and D. Hands together

You may also wish to start with steps 3 and 4 and follow them with 1 and 2.

A, B, C, and D. Hands together

E and F. Right hand

G and H. Left hand

E and G. Hands together

F and H. Hands together

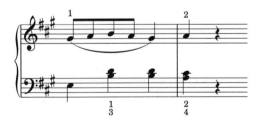

E, F, G, and H. Hands together

A–H. Entire excerpt

German Dance

Ludwig van Beethoven (1770-1827)

To create the conditions for flow to emerge, it is suggested that you not attempt to learn any section until the previous section has reached or almost reached the autonomous phase and until you are in flow. Deliberate attempts at evoking this state through monitoring your reactions will enhance your practice session, resulting in greater concentration, loss of self-consciousness, and surer internalization of the music, all of which are important characteristics of flow.

ENHANCING MOMENT-TO-MOMENT DECISIONS VIA THE FLOW/MASTERY FORM

Let's revisit the three Power Steps for Learning (PSLs), since successful learners have developed the ability to create an engine for continuous learning:

1. They know how to choose learning goals.
2. They reflect on learning strategies.
3. They are conscious of how to sustain motivation.

In order to ensure that you continually employ the three PSLs, I have created the Flow/Mastery Form (figure 5.1) to help you organize your piano practice so that you do not choose segments that are either too hard, which will cause frustration and/or anxiety, or too easy, which can cause boredom. By using the form to rate yourself often while you practice, you will avoid frustration, anxiety, and boredom.

```
Name of piece you are working on_____

Segment on which you are working_____

    (1)  Using the scales below, rate your stage of mastery:
Cognitive Stage          Associative Stage        Autonomous Stage
|-------------|------------------------------------------|------------|
             (2)  How challenging is this segment?
    Not hard                  Not so bad                  Very hard
    |-----------------------------------------------------------|
                    (3)  Were you having fun?
    No way!                  Starting to          Yes, this is awesome!
    |-----------------------------------------------------------|
       (4)  How would you rate your skill level during this interval?

    Very low                   Moderate                   Very high
    |-----------------------------------------------------------|
```

Figure 5.1 Flow/Mastery Form

The Flow/Mastery Form will help you to reflect on your practice. Filling out this form as you practice will help you ascertain your level of expertise for potential learning, enjoyment, and the absence of frustration and boredom (or, in other words, the crucial proper matching of skill and challenge). Continually giving thought to these elements will help inform your choice of segments. Once equipped with this knowledge, you should be better able to decide whether to start a new segment, remain on the current segment for a longer period, or subdivide the segment into subsegments that are less complex. Through the use of this form, you should gradually learn to make decisions that will increase the effectiveness of your practice.

Try the following procedure. At the beginning of each segment, fill out a Flow/Mastery Form and compare where you are after mastery begins to emerge. After five to ten minutes, rate yourself again. Repeat this procedure until skill and mastery are high and challenge is low. At this point, it is time to move on to another segment, or you will run the risk of becoming bored. Also, if at any point you decide that your enjoyment of the segment is low (question 3), it is definitely time to move to another segment. After you have been using this form for a while, your practicing will improve to the point where you will no longer need to use it.

MINDFUL REPETITION

Massive repetition as a practice technique is not only endorsed by Fitts and Posner as an essential part of the associative stage of their phases of learning, but it is also widely recognized by most pianists as an integral part of their daily routine. Repetition alone, however, can have little or no effect if it is mindless. You must pay attention both to your mental state and to the smallest touch and detail of tone. If either of these attentions is not present, you are likely to become either bored or frustrated, and small problems will surely develop beneath the level of your awareness. The problem may seem small, such as using the wrong finger or performing the passage with the slightly wrong nuance. It may also be as large as playing with a harsh, inappropriate tone or inaccurate execution of the notes.

The antidote to this style of practice is to be mindful of the smallest detail. Try to be aware of the gesture that exists between the notes by realizing that the playing of every note has two parts: preparation and execution. For instance, in the case of inaccuracies, realize that wrong notes or inappropriate tone could be a result of poor mental decoding or a preparatory elevating action that results in a descent onto the wrong note or a key strike that creates an inappropriately weak or strong tone. In other words, the deficit is of either attention or coordination.

In order to sort this out, try to make the distinction between faulty thinking and faulty actions (it may often be both). In the case of the former, write in a critical feature, such as a fingering or a dynamic, or even a reminder that may use words, such as "release to the left" or "be sure to use a vigorous staccato." In the case of a faulty action, rehearse the desired action until it becomes effortless and beautiful. I find that asking whether the action has become "fun and easy" usually helps to ascertain whether a passage has truly been mastered. These changes often occur only after you have repeated the pattern perhaps dozens of times, continually making the requisite mental and physical adjustments until the goal has been achieved.

CUSTOMIZING YOUR PRACTICE

Once you are in flow, you may experience a sense of heightened awareness that leads you to practice in a manner that differs from what has been described above. You may wish to alter the sequence of learning as a result of your excitement about what you have achieved. This type of experimentation should be encouraged. Once you are in flow, your creative impulses should guide your efforts and may in fact lead you away from the sequence of steps described above. Often, this will mean that you will be able to intuit or anticipate what step is to be taken next. This "self-tailoring" to one's own needs is of great importance, since this is how you will discover your own optimal procedure for learning.

CHAPTER 6

Learning a More Complex Piece

In chapter 5, I discussed the various procedures that would enable you to go into a state of flow while studying a simple piece such as the German Dance in A Major by Beethoven. You may recall that monitoring your reactions while studying the piece was essential to facilitating the flow state. This time, I would like to take a look at a somewhat more difficult composition. The principles we have already discussed will now be applied to the Waltz in C-sharp Minor, op. 64, no. 2, by Frederic Chopin. This piece contains quite a few learning units that we will examine for their relative degrees of challenge. The hope, of course, is to provide sufficient learning units allowing you to find appropriate segments to match your ability.

As you prepare to work on this waltz, it is highly advisable that you first read through the entire piece, making mental notes about what seems to work easily or what you feel will require more in-depth practicing. After doing so, peruse the excerpts that follow for the purpose of determining which one has the greatest potential to provide you with a flow experience as you learn the piece. You will most likely not go through the entire chapter chronologically. In fact, it is advisable in most cases that you not do so. Recall that flow occurs when the challenge that you take on is at or slightly above your perceived skill level relative to the chosen practice excerpt. When you have identified a properly matched excerpt, read the associated narrative below and then, and only then, begin practicing.

At this point, you may be wondering how you will know when it might be appropriate for you to tackle another practice unit or excerpt. Remember that as you are moving toward mastery, you will pass through three stages: the cognitive stage, the associative stage, and the autonomous stage. You should not move to another excerpt until you feel you have reached or almost reached the autonomous stage. By this point, most of the aspects of the excerpts will have become automatic, flowing, and basically effortless, and if you were to continue practicing the excerpt, it may become boring for you and hence flow-inhibiting. Remember that first and foremost, we are attempting to create conditions in which maximal enjoyment and concentration may exist at the same time. Most important, keep in mind that learning this piece in association with the flow state will render it ready for performance. Since the flow state leaves no room for self-consciousness or worry, your performance should be one of great beauty, clarity, control, and mastery.

À Madame Nathaniel de Rothschild

Valse

F. Chopin Op. 64 No. 2

The learning units described below are geared toward intermediate pianists. I will present them according to varying levels of complexity, as I did with the *German Dance* in chapter 5. There are three distinct sections in this waltz (the remainder of the piece consists of repetitions of these sections), and I will deal with each of the first three sections separately. As stated earlier, you should feel free to start your learning on any of the sections and with any segment. For organizational purposes, I advise that you start with one section and persist with that one until it is mastered. If, however, you feel capable of keeping track of your learning, making sure that you don't skip any segments, then you may start on any of the three sections and proceed to a new segment of your choosing even if it's in another section. While I don't recommend this approach, it should be acceptable as long as the main goal of constantly matching challenge with skill is achieved. The excerpts presented here may be learned out of order, depending on the skill/challenge self-assessments of the reader. This suggests that you only work on excerpts that are slightly above your self-perceived ability. This may mean, in fact, that you might wish to commence with hands-together work earlier in the learning process than is presented here. Where this is the case, you may skip to "Putting Hands Together" below.

A WORD ON PEDALING

I am sure that you have many thoughts regarding use of the pedal. As you are probably aware, when you depress the pedal, all the overtones related to the depressed keys will vibrate. Press the pedal all the way down, and the strings will vibrate unencumbered. Pressing the pedal just a fraction will simply loosen the dampers and impede the full vibration of the strings while at the same time giving them a little freedom. It is somewhere between these two extremes that you must exert the pedal. During the first measure of this Chopin piece, there is only one chord: C-sharp minor. You may choose, because of this, to depress the pedal all the way to the bottom. However, some of you may feel that holding the pedal for all three beats is excessive, so you might wish to hold it for only two beats, which will give you the opportunity to play the last beat without the accompanying overtones. This is an aesthetic decision that you must come to through experiment.

The typical advice during scalar passages as in measure 14

is not to use the pedal at all. My personal preference is to differ in this case, by pedaling through the entire measure. Because this is in a fairly high register, the available overtones above the melody are relatively few. Nevertheless, a certain amount of muddiness is inevitable in this highly chromatic passage if you follow this pedaling designation. The purists among us would allow no pedal at all. Yet there may be a middle road that preserves clarity even with some overtones. I am, of course, referring to the fact that between no pedal at all and depressing the pedal all the way to the bottom, there are many middle roads. Take a peek at the dampers. If you press the pedal very slowly, you'll see that the dampers hardly move. Yet there is still a little freedom for the strings and their accompanying overtones to be activated. I have heard it argued that the pedal has eight positions. One can argue that there are even more than this. Therefore, there is surely a position that satisfies every aesthetic. Again, it is up to you to experiment so you can be true to your own artistic decisions. As you go through the following text, you may wish to follow these pedalings. You may also wish to modify them according to your own desires. I would urge you to be true to your artistic sensibility, making sure that your artistic intentions are being nurtured and validated.

I will now describe in minute detail how you may go about learning the many practice units that can be extracted from this waltz. This list, of course, is not exhaustive; you may come up with many different combinations of your own. I would encourage you to make sure that when you rehearse each unit, it is learned in a manner that avoids both physical and mental stress and the two antiflow elements of boredom and frustration. You can derive physical, mental, and, above all, musical enjoyment from any of these practice units. Since the goal is for you to experience the heightened sense of concentration that accompanies the flow state, it is important that you fascinate yourself with your learning.

I present the following learning units in the order in which they appear in the music, since this may be the easiest organizational approach for you. Individual learning styles will vary, and you need not adhere to a strict chronological learning of these units, since sometimes you are ready for one learning unit but not the next one in the piece. You must have faith that by carefully absorbing each learning unit according to your perception of your own ability, the entire piece will eventually unfold.

PRACTICE UNITS AND THEIR CHALLENGES IN THE CHOPIN WALTZ IN C-SHARP MINOR
Main Left-Hand Challenges
Entire Piece

We will first address the left-hand challenges, beginning with the first full measure; because of the similarity of the left hand throughout the waltz, these challenges may be discussed globally.

(Video 1) ◀

Propelling the hand from the lower to the middle register requires a "push-off" on the first note of each measure, which in this case is C-sharp. The force you use in conjunction with this push-off and the resultant arc that is created will affect how you land. The combination of force and arc is known as *ballistics* (as in a ballistic missile). This type of challenge occurs throughout the piece, as the pattern of a single low note followed by two higher chords is used fairly consistently.

Both the ballistics from beats 1 to 2 and 3 to 1 and the topography of the landings will vary from measure to measure. *Topography* in this case refers to the ups and downs created by the black and white notes. If you think of the piano as a landscape, you will understand what this means. Visualizing scales may help with this concept. The C major scale, which is made up of only white notes, is flat, somewhat like the plains of Nebraska, whereas the F-sharp major scale, which is made up mainly of the raised black notes, may be likened to Colorado with its Rockies. All piano music requires varying combinations of white and black notes, creating a vast array of topographies. From this point on, we will refer to this characteristic of piano playing as a *keyscape*.

Sometimes in this waltz, you will land on a white note (which is situated on a lower elevation of the keyboard) with your thumb and on a black note (which is on a higher plane) with one of the middle fingers (that is, 2, 3, or 4). This occurs, for example, in the first measure of the second line. Sometimes just the opposite will occur, with your thumb playing the black note and a middle finger playing a white note. An example of this occurs at measure 11, when your left hand plays F-sharp and B:

▶ (Video 2)

This keyscape will have an entirely different feel. Shaping the hand to con-form to this upon landing should take place during the travel arc from the lowest note (in this case, B). Every measure could, and most likely should, be practiced individually over and over so the ballistic and keyscape fea-tures can be learned. With each repetition, it is important to experiment with varying hand shapes and arm positions until you discover the ones that feel most natural given your unique physical structure. At times, you will have to travel a great distance, which will necessitate an increase in the speed and an alteration of the height of the arc. Such a situation occurs in measure 14,

▶ (Video 3)

where you must quickly travel almost two octaves between beats 1 and 2. Fortunately, the dynamic at that time should be forte or mezzoforte. The force you use in order to accomplish that dynamic level with your left pinkie will allow you to launch yourself in such as way as to be able to travel the requisite distance in an instant.

On Tone, Ease, and Forearm Rotation

It is worth mentioning at this point that every excerpt should be played with a beautiful tone and with a technical approach that is free of the slightest amount of tension. In order to accomplish this, it is essential that you attempt to use different arm angles and heights in order to accommodate the various keyscapes until you are convinced that the approach you are using is the freest and thus the most comfortable and effective one possible. Freeing the arm with rotational gestures that originate from the elbow either to the right or to the left often relieves tension while providing power. Try rotating the forearm with the above excerpt in which you play the C-sharp and F-double sharp with a gentle rotational gesture emanating from the elbow. The following excerpt is a case in point:

(Video 4) ◀

Prepare for playing the C-sharp by rotating the arm (initiating this action from the elbow) so that the left side of the left hand is lifted and the right side is beneath it. (*Initiating* here and elsewhere means "starting the motion.") Gently swing your fifth finger onto the C-sharp and follow through slightly. The follow-through, if done well, will gently raise the thumb so the right side of the hand is now above the left side. Using the low C-sharp as a pivot point, carefully throw your hand to the chord on the second beat, landing in a nonpercussive manner in which the tone is beautiful and full. This pendulum process may be applied to the subsequent single notes and chords and in all similar passages.

Special Challenges Pertaining to Measure 65 – Third section in D-flat major

The main challenge of section 3 of the waltz is that Chopin here relaxes the strict *oom-pah-pah* rhythm of the previous two sections and treats the left hand far more melodically. The learning units I have selected from this section illustrate this:

In measure 65, Chopin states the left-hand standard waltz accompaniment as he did previously. In measure 66, however, something interesting occurs. Instead of beginning this measure with a low note, he simply holds the third beat over from the previous measure. On the third beat, the bottom note moves up a half step to A-natural, which in turn is held over the bar line as the fifth finger begins the third measure with D-flat. The challenge here is in the rhythmic variation and especially in the pivoting motion that occurs between beat 3 of the second measure and beat 1 of the third. It may be advisable, therefore, to become comfortable with just those two beats:

Once this transition is easy, I would suggest backing up one beat and mastering this segment:

Once the sound moves fluently through these three beats and you have found the right angle and the proper tone, it would then be advisable to move through the entire excerpt:

The wonderful thing about these measures is how Chopin creates a baseline from what was seemingly the bottom note of the tenor chord. Thus, the A-flat, which sounded like a member of the tenor chords (which, of course, was established during the first two sections), has now become a bass note that travels from A-flat to A-natural and then splits off to D-flat while it is being held over the bar line. This duality of the tenor becoming the bass and then again becoming the tenor is delicious, and the weight and hence voicing of the bottom of your left hand should reflect the desire to exploit this movement. Making this your goal will occupy you for quite a while, providing you with a very interesting but accessible challenge. Once this is mastered naturally, it will be necessary to move on to a new excerpt that will provide further challenge.

In measure 67, moving to the B-flat/F interval involves angling your arm in such a manner that makes it possible for you to play the two notes with your first and second fingers. To accomplish this in a stress-free manner and in a manner that does not compromise your tone, move your elbow toward your torso and play your thumb at a fairly high angle.

The D-flat and the D-natural that are played by the fifth finger in the measure 68 may puzzle you at first glance, since you may ascertain that the F in the tenor voice has to be held. On closer inspection, you will see that Chopin has marked this as a quarter note, which allows most hands to swing the arm to have the fifth finger land on the D-flat. If your hand is not big enough, try substituting the thumb for the second finger on the B-flat. Notice that after playing D-flat, the D-natural is easily played with the same fifth finger, as sliding from the D-flat to the D-natural is no problem. This enables the fourth finger to reach the E-flat, again, with little difficulty.

The challenge of measure 69 involves reaching the G-flat above middle C with the thumb. In order to stabilize this stretch so it doesn't cause too much difficulty, be sure to securely and solidly play the B-flat on the second beat, making it a base of support for the initiation of the action required to play the sixth on beat 3.

Combining Excerpts

The preceding excerpts should be combined once each of them has been learned to satisfaction. Remember that learning the individual excerpts should involve playing each of them in a manner that produces a beautiful tone and is free of stress. When combining the first two excerpts, for instance,

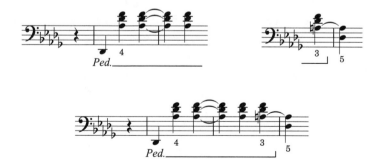

do not assume that because each of the excerpts alone has been learned well individually, it will result in your being able to combine both excerpts satisfactorily. Transitions between excerpts are often challenging and may become the cause of tension. The approach to the second excerpt via the first excerpt is, therefore, crucial. To lessen the difficulties that may occur between excerpts, it may be necessary to practice a transitional excerpt consisting of the ending of the first excerpt and the beginning of the second:

▶ (Video 8)

It is essential that you learn to create hybrid excerpts in order to smooth over transitions and create excerpts of increasing size. Small excerpts must become larger excerpts, which in turn become entire sections. Once the sections are combined sufficiently, you will have learned an entire piece.

Main Right-Hand Challenges
First Section-First System

Tempo giusto

▶ (Video 9)

One of the main challenges you will face with the opening to the waltz is getting the F-double-sharp and the D-sharp to sound precisely together. Experiment with varying hand heights and arm angles until you feel that you can project the top two notes (the E and the D-sharp) with a lovely tone and a slight diminuendo into the D-sharp so it emulates a sigh. While subordinate to the top two notes, the G-sharp and the F-double-sharp should also simultaneously suggest their own proportionate diminuendo.

Initiate the action by swinging slightly to the left with the second finger, which should raise the pinkie side of the hand somewhat. Carefully lower the raised pinkie onto the E. Repeat this gesture several times until the arm and the hand are comfortable and perfectly synchronized and so you achieve the desired tone.

 (Videos 10 and 11)

The two black notes here at the beginning of measure 3 must be played in a way that allows the grace note B to be played cleanly before the A/F-sharp third. If you play the grace note by leaning your forearm ever so slightly to the right, you should then be able to lift the thumb from the F-sharp, which will facilitate its subsequent repetition.

 (Videos 12 and 13)

In the second half of measure 3, the G-sharp/F-natural major second must be repeated clearly. It is important that you also emphasize the dissonance of the second resolving into the more consonant sixth. Initiate the action by leaning a little bit more on the G-sharp than on the F-natural so the soprano may project to the D-sharp.

 (Videos 14 and 15)

For the end of measure 4, using fingers 3/2 (rather than 2/1) on the G-sharp/F-sharp second will facilitate playing the C-sharp/E sixth with 5/1 and maintaining a legato line. Keep in mind that it will be essential for you to lean into the soprano notes, making sure that they sing out. In this case, the keyscape is quite easy, as both notes are black and hence on the same plane. Since you are playing with the longer and stronger third finger on the G-sharp, it should be fairly easy to project that note. Rehearse the gesture until both the G-sharp and the C-sharp ring out beautifully. Note that as in the previous measure, there is a dissonant second resolving to a more consonant sixth. Rehearse this until it is comfortable and clear. You may have to play with different angles and experiment with different fingerings. In addition, both power and the release of tension may be attained by using a small forearm rotational gesture to the left side for the G-sharp/F-sharp second.

Joining Excerpts Together

The two rests in each measure should act as a rhythmic trigger to initiate and send the hand. A feeling of restarting for the second pair in each measure should provide sufficient impetus for its realization. Using a larger gesture will enable you to make a full-bodied crescendo to the end of the measure.

At this point, you may wish to begin combining hands, even if for only the first two measures. If so, read ahead to "Putting Hands Together."

Second System

▶ (Video 16)

At the beginning of measure 7, as before, you will need to lean a little to the right to project the top note of the opening second. As both notes are white, this should present little difficulty. Again, the grace note, in this case the G-sharp, can function in a way that can lift your hand, enabling the finger playing the D to rise to the surface quickly enough so it may be repeated.

▶ (Videos 17 and 18)

You have prepared for the end of measure 7 already. Because these four notes are all white in topography, you may use the comments above pertaining to the latter part of measure three, as all those notes are black and thus similar in terms of shape.

(Video 19)

First, make sure that all the notes within the three-note chord at the start of measure 9 are played simultaneously. Then, after playing the G-sharp, initiating from the elbow, lean your forearm arm a little to the right, which will allow your thumb to come onto the E. You should then lean on the thumb again, this time to the left, which will lift the right side of your arm slightly and allow you to play the G-sharp again. In other words, for the G-sharp/E/G-sharp combination, you will be leaning to the left for the E and to the right for the second G-sharp. This pendular motion should initiate from the elbow, which should be flexible and unconstrained.

(Videos 20 and 21)

The initial move of the thumb is to the left. This sets in motion a left-right pendular sequence of forearm swings as the second and third fingers alternate playing, culminating in the chord on measure 11. You should experiment with the amplitude of the swings so they feel utterly comfortable and balanced upon landing and the follow-through allows you to swing in the opposite direction for the next note. In order to enhance the crescendo, you should gradually increase the weight on each individual repeated note until you reach the chord, which should sound robust.

(Videos 22 and 23)

The types of challenges that exist in measures 12–16 have largely been covered already. Note the left-right swings, which will help you play this passage. The amplitude of the forearm swings should increase and decrease in order to coincide with the crescendo in measures 12–13 and the diminuendo during measures 14–16.

▶ (Videos 24 and 25)

Chopin writes an inverted mordent in measure 30, which merits special consideration. A string of three back-and-forth swings will help you accomplish this embellishment. Initiate the inverted mordent (composed of the notes F-sharp, G-sharp, F-sharp) with a forearm rotation to the left for the F-sharp, which will swing your arm back to the right for the G-sharp, and then in turn swing your arm back to the left for the second F-sharp. A possible new challenge occurs between the third beat of measure 30 and the first two beats of measure 31. You may find that the F-sharp, F-double-sharp, G-sharp sequence leaves your hand feeling cramped. If you have large fingers, you may find it difficult to negotiate the F-double-sharp, in that your third finger may get stuck between the two black notes (no fun). The best way to remedy this is to allow your arm to come out for the F-sharp so you may play it right on the edge with the second finger. Continuing to bring your arm out for the next note will allow your third finger to play the F-double-sharp in the white area of the key, thus mitigating the cramped feeling somewhat. During the sequence of notes, it is important that your hand remain comfortable and not clutch.

In order to play the next two notes, both G-sharps but in different registers, it will be necessary to go back in toward the fallboard for the next two notes with the arm so you may play the first G-sharp with the fourth finger and then an octave lower with the thumb. In other words, in order to feel open and uncramped, go out for the first two notes and back in for the next two.

Second Section

With its familiar lovely, winding, and curving musical shape, the second page contains passagework that is delightful yet a bit more complex than you might first assume.

▶ (Video 26)

For the pickup to measure 33, begin with a forearm swing to the left, leaning on and pivoting with your thumb. Make sure that just the right amount of your thumb covers the G-sharp so you feel secure. Too much thumb will leave you feeling slightly immobile, making it difficult to play the following note. Too little will make it difficult to use the key to plant your thumb in order to throw your forearm back to the right with your fourth finger.

The throwback to the fourth finger starts an elliptical *under* shape with the forearm that peaks on the A with the fifth finger. This note then becomes the first note of the circular *over* shape that continues through the end of the measure.

It is important to experiment with the amplitudes of both the under shape and the over shape so they are neither too large nor too small. The topography of the passage is a little tricky since the pinkie on the A has to be placed just right so it will support the forearm as it transitions from an under shape to an over shape. It is a good idea to practice this one measure until you feel as if you are ice skating securely, with perfect balance and with a beautiful tone on each note.

Enjoy practicing these and the similar passages on this section, as they are highly pianistic and should provide both kinestheic and aural gratification.

(Videos 27 and 28) ◀

Superficially, the measures from 34 through the beginning of 37 look just like the ones we have just discussed. However, there are subtle differences in the keyscape because of the ever-changing combinations of black notes and white notes. The first two of these measures are a bit easier than the third, because the second note, which is the turnaround note, is black. This means that the arm will be slightly raised, making it easier to complete the over shape. You might find measure 35 slightly more challenging than 34, since the music here proceeds from a white note to a black note. This is mitigated somewhat by the fact that the longer fourth finger plays the white note. You should be easily able to find the correct gesture, since the shorter fifth finger should almost be on top of the F-sharp. Measure 36 is similar to 33, in that the keyscape of the measure begins black to white. Do not assume that you can use identical gestures in measure 33 and measure 37, as each one has subtle differences arising from the varying keyscapes. Each should be practiced independently as many times as needed in order to learn the exact size and shape of the ellipse that your forearm seems to prefer. Once you are familiar with this, you can practice two to four measures at a time.

▶ (Videos 29 and 30)

Because the over shape has been reduced from five to four notes in measures 37 through the beginning of 39, you must adjust the shape of the gesture accordingly. The next over shape has been interrupted with a repeated note in both of these measures. When playing from measure 37 to 38, complete the first of the two with a swing to the right, and make an intermediate swing to the left for the second note. Measure 38 is completed with a swing to the right on the last note. Another swing to the left occurs in measure 39 for the G-sharp.

At measure 39 and the beginning of 40, the under shape has now become four notes long, so again, you must adjust the gesture accordingly. The real difficulty comes at the turnaround note A, after which you must play G-sharp and then F-double-sharp. Again, your hand may be in danger of becoming cramped, because in rapid succession, you must play finger 5 on a white note, 3 on a black note, and then 1 on a white note. A possible solution to this is to play the black note about an inch from the edge, which will create sufficient space for your thumb to land comfortably. Naturally, each hand is different, so you will have to experiment to see what works for you. You should not be afraid to play the third finger toward the fallboard in order to create space for the thumb.

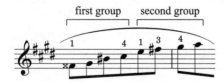

▶ (Video 31)

When practicing runs, it is often advisable to isolate the groups that begin with the thumb and master each of them individually. There are two such thumb groups in the jagged scale passage in measures 40 and 41. The first four notes make up the first group, and the last four notes make up the second. In the first group, getting from the G-sharp to the B-sharp is a little tricky, in that it involves a major-third skip shifting from a black key to a white key that needs to be accomplished between fingers 2 and 3. An inward motion with the arm will help facilitate this. The next group culminates with the fifth finger on A, which, as before, functions as the turnaround note for the ensuing over shape:

Practice each thumb group separately until you find the right gesture in which each note feels comfortable. Perhaps the trickiest part of the eight notes in these two groups is crossing the thumb quickly under the hand to get from the fourth note C-sharp to the E. It is advisable to decide first how to comfortably play the second group of four notes so that when you approach the E from the C-sharp, it is positioned at approximately the same angle as when those four notes are played as a separate unit. Once you know how to play the second unit comfortably, try to use the same initial gesture with the thumb on the E when you play the full eight-note passage.

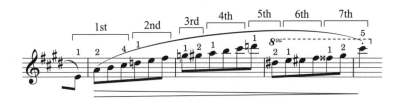

This excerpt, from the end of measure 44 through the beginning of measure 48, is made up of seven thumb groups. Each unit's keyscape varies, consisting of between two and four combinations of black and white notes. As the keyscape of each unit varies, it is advisable to make sure that each of these is comfortable by itself before you string them together. Each unit initiates with a white note and ends with a black note. Be sure to place the thumb well on each of the following units so that it easily allows an inward movement of the arm to accommodate the black notes.

(Video 32)

The arm should move in toward the C-sharp, which is played with the fourth finger.

(Video 33)

The arm should move in toward the F-sharp, which is played with the third finger.

(Video 34)

After playing the third finger in the previous excerpt, angle the forearm to enable a comfortable swing to the right. The thumb can then act as a pivot to enable a forearm swing to the opposite direction (left), which will allow the third finger to comfortably play the G-sharp. This in turn will allow the thumb to swing right in order to play the A in the next excerpt.

Move the forearm in toward the C-sharp.

Proceed as in the third thumb group described above.

Proceed as in the fourth thumb group described above.

(Video 35)

Sit securely and well (but not too solidly, or you'll get stuck), with the second finger on the G-sharp so you can throw your fourth or fifth finger to the right. If you bring your elbow slightly in, you will lessen the possibility of missing, which should add to your confidence. Choose a beautiful rich, ringing tone to conclude this climactic passage.

Section 3

The darker and more haunting mood of the previous two sections in C-sharp minor now gives way to the more lyrical and rhythmically spacious section in the parallel major key of D-flat major.

The lovely first phrase, from the end of measure 64 through the beginning of measure 69, is subdividable into two parts.

(Video 36) ◀

Begin the first part with a forearm swing to the left, landing well with the thumb so you may then swing in the opposite direction and affect a beautiful tone an octave higher with the pinkie. There is plenty of time to choose your tone and accompanying gestures for both the F and the E-flat.

(Video 37) ◀

Starting with the C in measure 68, a string of right, left, right, and left forearm swings occurs. Go in a little with your arm to the G-flat. Recall that when crossing over your thumb (as in the case of going from the C to the B-flat here), it is possible to approach the note directly from the right or by passing the note by a fraction and then swinging right. The latter approach, while appearing somewhat more complex, will ultimately produce a fuller tone, as it will better enable the arm to be comfortably repositioned over the B-flat, allowing for a surer path to the ensuing F.

Starting with the pickup to measure 65, a series of leaps to a high note occurs at the beginning of each phrase. Subsequent leaps occur at measures 70 and 73 and the pickup to measure 76. Each of these leaps is higher than the one before, with the D-flat in measure 75 being the highest and the most climactic. Each of these leaps should be played with a forearm swing to the right of increasing size and intensity. In order for the overall line to be clear, the two D-flats that occur here should be preceded by the largest swings of all. Be sure that the sound is bell-like, unforced, penetrating, and, above all, gorgeous.

▶ (Video 38)

Measure 84 involves playing eight even eighth notes in the meter of 3/4, which is not a logical ratio to subdivide mentally. Assuming that the approximate tempo of this section is 120 beats per minute to the quarter note, or somewhat above, will allow us to address this issue. Since the quarter note is at 120, the dotted half, or the tempo of each downbeat, would be 40. While the metronome is ticking at this very slow tempo, attempt to fit all eight notes evenly into this space. Make sure the downbeats of measures 84 and 85 occur on the beat. Now listen carefully to make sure that all the other notes fit in evenly. It is helpful to use an over shape for the first three notes, which are then followed by an under shape through the G, a small over shape through the F, and then a small under shape to the B-flat. The passage finishes with an over shape through the A-flat.

Putting Hands Together

This hands-together discussion appears here after discussions of learning excerpts of increasing size with hands separate. This is simply because interspersing discussions of hand-separate work with hands-together work might prove overly confusing. Yet there is no reason to assume that this is the best way to proceed; the reader may wish to put hands together earlier in the learning process. In order to maintain the flow state, remember that your desire should be to constantly monitor your reactions to what you are doing so that you can choose challenges that are closely matched to your perceived skill.

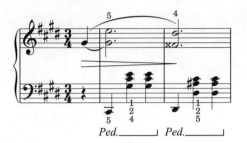

Ped.⌐⌐⌐⌐⌐⌐⌐┘ Ped.⌐⌐⌐⌐⌐⌐⌐┘ (Video 39)

Starting at the very beginning, the initiating G-sharp should be perceived as triggering the simultaneous move to the E in the right hand and the C-sharp in the left hand. Feel the effect of playing both fifth fingers together, making sure your arms feel balanced and the tone is rich (especially in the melodic right hand). As stated above, use the C-sharp to push off the left arm in order to land effortlessly on the chords two octaves above. As with the first note of the piece, the second chord should be perceived as going both to the D-sharp/F-double-sharp sixth in the right hand and the D-sharp in the left hand. Again, take care that you have a feeling of balance between the arms and that the top note of the right hand is projected. As with the first measure, the low note in the left hand should be used to push off in order to arrive gracefully on the chords above.

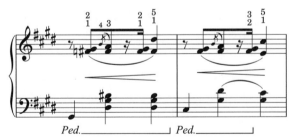

Ped.⌐⌐⌐⌐⌐⌐⌐⌐⌐⌐⌐┘ Ped.⌐⌐⌐⌐⌐⌐⌐┘ (Videos 40 and 41)

The G-sharp in the left hand of measure 3 starts a series of chain reactions. It triggers the G-sharp/F-natural thumb-side rotational gesture to the second finger of the right hand, which in turn triggers the grace note to the pinkie-side B. The B then simultaneously triggers the F-sharp/A third in the right hand and the left-hand chord. It is important to feel the simultaneous arrival of both elements on the second beat. It is interesting that on the second beat, the two notes in the right hand and the three notes the left hand may be thought of as being approached rotationally to the thumb side of both hands. Practice this until you feel that the soprano note is being projected with a beautiful tone and that the chord in the left hand is subordinate to the melody in the right hand.

Now put these two excerpts (measures 1–4) together:

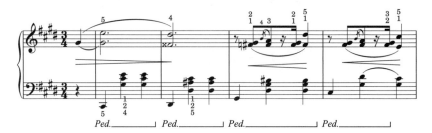

In order to do so, you may have to work a bit on this two-beat passage, which is the connector between the two excerpts:

It may be wise to feel the chord as a pickup. Pickups have a tendency to propel to the downbeat, so thinking in this manner may facilitate the binding together of these two excerpts.

As in measures 1 and 2, in measures 5 and 6, the tone must be full for the two notes that are played with the right pinkie. Be sure to observe the symmetry and balance between the two pinkies on the downbeat.

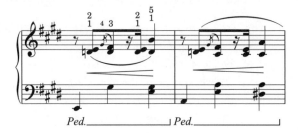

The keyscape issues that are present in measures 7 and 8 are similar to those in measures 3 and 4. However, the challenges are not quite as demanding, because in measure 7, both hands proceed from the greater surface area provided by white notes (E in the left hand and E/D in the right hand), coupled with the thinning of the texture in the left hand on beats 2 and 3. Just as in measures 3 and 4, the triggering gestures of the left hand to the right hand are both to the left side (pinkie side, left hand; thumb side, right hand). The demands are similar for measure 8.

In order to bridge these two excerpts (measures 5–8), it again may be a good idea to perceive the last beat of the first excerpt as the pickup to the first beat of the second excerpt:

In this case, initiate action by rotating the left forearm to the right on A/F-sharp, which will in turn cause a swing to the low E. This will then trigger the chain reaction as described above (measures 9–10):

Now put the above two excerpts (measures 7–10) together:

As we have seen, despite the fact that it is the ending chord of the previous musical idea, it is nevertheless a good idea to practice this chord as if it is the pickup to measure 9 in order to link the two measures physically:

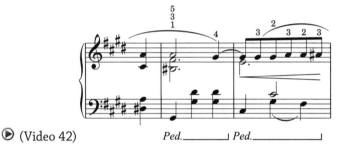

▶ (Video 42)

You should feel a physical connection from the center of your right palm straight to your elbow for both chords. The release from the chord on the third beat in your left hand should be to the thumb side, causing the left side of your left hand to lift a little. Using your thumb as a pivot point, you can then throw your arm to the next G-sharp, which may be played with either the fourth or the fifth finger. Enjoy the resultant buoyant yet solid feeling for both chords with a slight emphasis on the second chord.

While the right hand holds the chord, the left hand must now pivot on and follow through past the G-sharp in order to immediately return to the middle of the piano, where it plays the two-note chord on the second beat (D-sharp/G-sharp). Again, it is important for both arms to feel settled on the downbeat of measure 10. The right arm then rotates to the notes G-sharp (tiny right swing), G-sharp (tiny left swing), A (tiny right swing), A (tiny left swing), and A-sharp (tiny right swing). Simultaneously, the left arm must swing from the C-sharp in order to leap to the two-note chord, C-sharp/G-sharp on beat 2. Note that the right-hand swing on beat 2 is a swing to the left, while the left arm is swinging to the right. Thus, both arms swing toward each other simultaneously. It is essential that the causal effect of each hand's previous note (G-sharp in the right and C-sharp in the left) be fully felt. In order to do this, it may be necessary to practice these two beats several times until both palms can comfortably land securely and flat on the second beat. Finish learning the measure once a feeling of security has been gained on the second beat.

This passage has been described earlier, when it was examined with separate hands. The three bass notes that occur on the downbeats of measures 13, 14, and 15 provide harmonic punch to the chromatic line of the right hand. The last notes of measures 12, 13, and 14 in the right hand may be thought of as pickups to the following measures. Doing so will add to this passage's drive. The first of these,

Ped._____   (Video 43)

is initiated by rotating the forearm to the right in order to play the first of the two C-double-sharps. Using a pendular forearm action, the second C-double-sharp would then be played to the left with the thumb. You might find it useful to think of this very action as a way to trigger your left pinkie to the D-sharp. So in this scenario, the first C-double-sharp (the pickup note) in the right hand triggers both the second C-double-sharp to the left and the left hand's D-sharp on the downbeat, also to the left. The parallel action of both arms is a wonderful way to power the upcoming crescendo accompanied by the left hand's full-bodied chord on the second beat.

The following two measures,

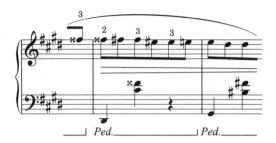

are similar but not exactly the same, in that the right arm is initiated by the second finger to the left on the pickup eighth note and then to the right with the third finger on the downbeat.

The main complication in measure 31 involves playing the right thumb (G-sharp) in the middle of two left-hand notes (C-sharp/E) on the second beat. In order to accomplish this, it is important to create enough space under the left hand so the right thumb can fit. Imagine that you are creating a cave-like shape with your left hand, which should puff up sufficiently so your right hand has plenty of room. When launching from the previous G-sharp in the left hand, it is important to make sure that you do not come crashing down on the second beat. The G-sharp in the right hand is, after all, the melody note. It is a good idea to "trampoline" (that is, play it over and over) on the second beat's chord in order to seek and choose the balance and gesture that feel and sound right while projecting the inner G-sharp melodically.

Section 1 Wrap-up

At this point, you may choose to go on to section 2, or you may choose to review what you have learned in section 1, which at this point has been dealt with extensively and thoroughly. Play through the entire section, carefully noting the passages that are nearly or fully automatic. Also note those passages that seem awkward or where inaccuracies or poor tones still persist. The former passages will allow you artistic free-dom. They should also provide an ease in execution that you should find enjoyable. Those passages that are less than automatic and where there is still struggle will seem inflexible. You may also note that you physically tense up when you attempt to play them. It is a wonderful idea to go back and ask yourself why this is happening. Do not be tempted just to "run it" over and over again in the hope that providence or some force outside you will eventually drop it down on you. Answering the question of why you are uncomfortable—whether it is physical or musical—is vital to your improvement. It is advisable to go back to those excerpts and make sure that you are executing them in a way that is flowing musically, physically, and, perhaps most important, psychologically. As emphasized in earlier chapters, monitoring your reactions is crucial to your learning. Making sure that you are mindful of your own reactions in this stage of your development will provide the key to your improvement. Going into the psychological state of flow via this wonderful section of Chopin's waltz is the goal.

Putting Hands Together Section 2

Because of their similarity, the issues that pertain to this section may be dealt with globally. Each measure begins in the right hand with the over/under shape gesture above. The circular motion that facilitates this gesture throughout this section is in contrast to the somewhat jagged, bouncy gesture of the left hand. Recall that in the left-hand waltz gesture, the downbeat is played with sufficient energy, and then follow-through allows you to play the second beat with a tone by design and not by default. By this I mean that the ballistics that occur as a result of launching from the lower note must get you to the second beat in time so you can choose your tone. Some pianists create a secondary melody from the notes that occur on the second and third beats of each of these measures (33–37):

Others choose to ignore this opportunity. Since this repeats so many times, there are pianists who choose to do both versions during its various iterations. Whichever artistic choice you make does not change the fact that the left-hand gesture is decidedly different from that of the right hand.

If you were to tap your stomach in three different places consecutively while rubbing your head circularly, you would experience something like the challenges that must be overcome for playing this section to become second nature. As I mentioned when discussing each hand separately, the shape of the right-hand gesture keeps changing because of its ever-changing keyscape. At the same time, in the left hand, both the ballistics necessary to travel distances between the first beat and the second beat and its own keyscapes also change from measure to measure. So in order to execute this section well, you will need to be mindful of circles in the right hand and bounces in the left hand.

In order to become adept at this (after mastering each hand separately), it is a good idea to practice the first two beats of measure 33:

▶ (Video 44)   *Ped.*_____

Here the right hand's ellipse changes course from an under shape to an over shape, and the left hand travels from the low B-sharp to the middle register of the piano. Again, it bears repeating that the right arm describes the turnaround point of the ellipse in each measure just when the left hand leaps. Be mindful of the legato nature of the gesture in the right hand while the left hand pushes off in order to complete its leap. Once these two elements have been synchronized to your satisfaction and with a beautiful tone, it would be a good idea to practice the second and third beats:

▶ (Video 45)

Here the right hand finishes the over shape while the left hand repeats the chord. In this manner, the first six measures of the section may be learned.

The shape of measure 39 is slightly different from that of the previous ones. But it is easily accomplished, since there is an intervening rest between the low note and the chord in the left hand.

Proceeding to measure 40, since the right hand has two thumb groups, it is a good idea to be mindful of each of these in conjunction with the left hand. Therefore, become comfortable with beats 1 and 2 first, then the B-sharp all by itself, and then combining both of them. Be mindful of how the right hand and the left hand synchronize on the beats, making sure that the arrivals of the beats are absolutely simultaneous. Since most of the other issues in this section have already been covered, it is time to move on.

Section 3

Because of the slower tempo, longer note values in the right hand, and the generally peaceful nature of the left hand, it is safe to assume that many of the two-hand synchronization issues in this section are fairly straightforward. For the most part, it is highly advisable to be mindful of the synchronicity of both hands, making sure that the loveliness of the right-hand melody is never jeopardized by the left hand.

The notable exception to the simplicity of the synchronization issues occurs in measure 84, where the left hand and the right hand execute a polyrhythm of eight against three. You may choose to dodge this issue entirely by doing what some pianists do when playing this measure. And that is merely to play the first beat as a duple and the second and third beats as triplets. I am sure that the purists among you would be horrified at this solution, and, frankly, I put it here simply because there are recorded examples of this interpretation by fine pianists:

I personally do not advocate taking this approach without first learning the proper polyrhythmic solution, which in the right hand has already been dealt with. Synchronizing the first beat is actually quite easy, since both notes need to come down simultaneously on the downbeat. The third note of the right hand needs to occur just before the second note in the left hand; to accomplish this effect, it may be helpful to hear the E in the right hand as the trigger to the D-flat in the left. Similarly, the F, which is the sixth note in the right hand, must occur right *after* the D-flat in the left hand. It may, therefore, be useful to experience the D-natural in the left hand as a trigger to the F in the right. Overall, it is important that the tempo of this measure not be altered in any way to accommodate this polyrhythm in the early stage of learning. Eventually, your own artistic inclinations will help you decide if perhaps freedom of rubato is warranted here.

Finishing the Piece

You have now had a meticulous explanation of how you might approach the majority of the smaller challenges that exist in this piece. Having the patience to practice small units for the purpose of going into the flow state via each excerpt's potential for beauty, kinesthetic coordination, and opportunity for expression will result in your spending more time with each excerpt. When we are in the flow state, we simply want to stay in the flow state. When we are enjoying ourselves, we want to continue doing so. Like a master mason, you have now created the building blocks that can go into creating the mighty edifice, which will be learning the entire piece of music.

The principles that have been espoused up to now will hold true as you learn entire phrases, as these phrases become sections, and as the sections build to the entire piece. As the form of the piece is ABCBABA, some of you will wish to go about this systematically, with half of each large section becoming a goal (many editions of this waltz provide each major section as a full page, each of which in turn is divisible into two sections of three lines each). Others may wish to take larger sections or smaller sections. As I have said repeatedly throughout this chapter, creating your own excerpts for practice is key to learning. Naturally, repeating each excerpt over and over in a mindless manner is to be avoided at all costs. You are both the doer and the observer. By this I mean that you must continually assess your activity to make sure that your inner intentions are fulfilled. The remaining question, then, is how you know when your inner intentions are fulfilled?

THE JOY AND EXHILARATION OF DISCOVERY

Have you ever had the experience of riding in a car, perhaps in a place you have never been before, when just around the bend, you glimpse a sight so beautiful that you are startled into a state of wonder? I can vividly remember my first such experience when I was driving in Rome with my Italian uncle, whom I had met for the first time just the day before. I was only twenty years old and still feeling the effects of jet lag when the taxi we were riding in turned the corner to reveal the massive monument to Victor Emmanuel II—sometimes nicknamed "The Typewriter"—a structure my uncle hated. Of course, I had no idea of his feelings for the magnificent sight that greeted me. When I exclaimed "Che bella!" in my newly acquired Italian, he looked at me as if I were crazy and had no aesthetic sense—most likely attributed to my being from New Jersey and not Italia. Nevertheless, I remember feeling that the sight was extraordinary. I can also vividly recall my autonomic responses, in which my pulse quickened and my breathing was affected. I have experienced this kind of physiological response many times since; every time I behold something that I perceive as magnificent, such as the Grand Canyon or Notre Dame in Paris, I have a similar response. Similarly, when composing, I know I have solved my compositional issues when something akin to this response occurs. It also happens when I know I have explained something just right while teaching. I provide these personal stories as a way to provide a spark the reader, who undoubtedly has also experienced such wonders.

Something like what I've just described occurs when you have taken the building blocks that you have so carefully nurtured and mindfully put them together. Remember, if you are not going into the flow state or, more unfortunately, if you are feeling frustrated or bored, then your piecing together of your practicing excerpts is not being done well. This is the great art of practicing. Monitoring your own responses to what you are doing and then continually adjusting accordingly are essential to the emergence of your inner artist. This is also the way to find a unique interpretation, one that is free of the cookie-cutter approach that you so often hear, especially when learning popular pieces such as this Chopin waltz.

SUMMARY

This chapter has considered the Chopin waltz in minute detail. We have discussed respecting the importance of the tiny in the way a master craftsman honors the miniature section of a larger whole. We have seen that practice excerpts can be as small as two beats or even one chord. Sometimes the smallest units will provide you with the challenge necessary to immerse yourself in a skill-building activity. This activity will take you through the three phases of learning: cognitive (one continually gives instructions to oneself), associative (a mixture of automaticity and instruction giving), and autonomous (the gesture is mastered or learned; it has become automatic). Matching each challenge appropriately and continuously with your skill level will increase your chances of launching yourself into the flow state. Each unit, thus polished, can act as the building block for larger units, which in turn can provide the necessary stuff for again going into a state of flow. These larger units can then be united with other larger units successively until the entire piece itself may lead you into the flow state. Thus, flow will be psychologically, kinesthetically, and emotionally embedded within this wonderful piece.

Refer to the practice flow chart in chapter 4 (figure 4.7). As it shows, if the challenge is too great, the pianist should move to a simpler segment or perhaps subdivide the current segment into smaller, more digestible pieces. If the student's skill level is beyond the level of the challenge, then the student should continue practice until mastery of the segment is achieved at the autonomous phase of learning.

To reiterate something mentioned early in this chapter, learning this piece in association with the flow state has rendered it ready for performance. Since the flow state leaves no room for self-consciousness or worry, your performance should be one of great beauty, clarity, control, and mastery.

CHAPTER 7

Developing the Confidence
to Perform

Music is where I've experience that [enlightenment]. I'm in a flow, I'm in the zone, there's a definite shift in my consciousness, without desire, without my ego, without me thinking, oh wow, I'm playing great. Just experiencing it as a flowing, living moment. Once you've experienced it, you always know there's a place to go to.

Dimitri Ehrlich (1997, 240)

MY STORY OF CONFIDENCE

Many years ago, as a young pianist just out of college, I was asked to perform in a group piano recital of my colleagues at Montclair State College in New Jersey, where I had recently been hired as an adjunct professor. Being a reasonably experienced performer, I was nevertheless a bit anxious about performing with such superb and accomplished faculty members. About a day before the concert was to take place, I learned something that gave me further pause. Not only was I to perform with my incredibly erudite colleagues, but it so happened that my former teacher and distinguished concert artist Arminda Canteros was also going to perform in the recital. Although Arminda had been a wonderful and inspiring mentor, my insecurities got the best of me, and I began to have irrational visions of her disapproval accompanied by a steady succession of insecure thoughts, such as "If I had stayed with her a little longer, I might be playing at a higher level" or "Maybe I actually *should* have stayed with her a little longer." Arminda, a wonderfully warm Argentinian woman, was a superb performer and had just made her Carnegie Hall debut. In addition, at the time of the recital, she was one of the most sought-after teachers in New York and had worked with many professional pianists. I began to wonder if my decision to perform in this recital was actually a foolhardy one.

Fortunately, there was also a rational inner voice that motivated me to develop a plan of action in the midst of my near panic. Somehow I mustered the courage to ask Ms. Canteros if she would be kind enough to listen to me perform before the recital, and, throwing caution to the wind, I decided that I would give it my all. The piece I performed was the Capriccio from Ernő Dohnányi's *Four Pieces*, op. 2, a flashy, full-fisted, Late Romantic work in the style of Brahms. After playing the cascading interlocking octave passage that concludes the piece, I turned to Ms. Canteros and awaited her verdict (for it really seemed that I had asked her to become both my judge and jury). After no more than four or five seconds (which to me seemed like four or five minutes), she provided a response that was both beautiful in its simplicity and great in its capacity to raise my spirits. In her lovely Spanish-accented English, she proclaimed, "Oh, Tomé, that was be-u-tifool. You have trooly improved sow much! You never played like that when you stodied with me!" These words of praise demonstrated the generosity of spirit of the fabulous Arminda Canteros. Looking back, I realize that the first two sentences left alone could have seemed equivocal or too general to allay my fears, but the last sentence was the clincher that blossomed my confidence to overflowing. Her words were truly a gift, and I am happy to report that my performance, buoyed by her comments, was a wonderful success.

In retrospect, and knowing the wisdom of Arminda the mentor, I have no doubt that her words were carefully calculated to inspire self-esteem and generate the confidence within me to share the stage with her, not as her former student but as a colleague. It can be argued that this last interaction was in fact one of her greatest lessons with me. I am certain that at the time, it made me feel like a million bucks. In truth, I was well prepared, with every reason to feel confident, but it was Arminda who gave me permission to access my inner strength.

Over the decades, I have found both with my students and personally that willing yourself to have confidence through positive self-assertions or unsupported positive thinking is limited in its ability to provide the bedrock self-confidence necessary for performing, not only without fear but also with an eagerness for the experience. As I have just implied, in order to feel confident, you must be fully supported by effort and experience. As you get deeper and deeper into flow practicing, your practice procedures will gradually evolve. You will begin to discern what works and what doesn't. Over time, you will begin to understand that you absolutely can rely on your perceptions regarding practicing. Because you will have learned, via slow practicing, to make each practice session count, you, too, will learn to realize steady gains that are real and strong. Knowing that you can depend on yourself to unfailingly make the correct decisions regarding practice will seep deeper into your consciousness, providing you with an ever-increasing sense of self-belief. This self-belief will eventually provide you with the confidence necessary to perform. Again, keep in mind that it will take effort and experience. The resultant belief in your efficacy as a learner will give you the confidence to share with others. Performing well must be a continuation of what you accomplish while learning. Confidence is something you give yourself, or you don't get it.

GOAL PLANNING

In order to make a positive change, it is essential to create a daily practice plan that is reasonable, doable, and, above all, within your capabilities. It is important, therefore, that the practice goals you set are slightly above your perceived skill level, and it is also important to set an intention of creating the conditions necessary to go into the state of flow. Some people find it beneficial to set tomorrow's goals at the conclusion of today's practice session. There is something efficacious about sleeping on your intentions in order to give your subconscious mind the opportunity to internalize the goals for the next day.

When setting your goals, ask yourself if you really, truly want to do them or if they are a result of your thinking, "I *should* do this." Earlier, I described the tyranny of the word *should*. Your intention should be to achieve goals that have the potential to create flow and enjoyment in learning. If your goals cause any tension whatsoever, then you are probably choosing challenges that are beyond what you can accomplish. This is not to say that you cannot eventually work up to the more lofty goals you set for yourself. Remember that in order to create conditions for flow, you must be very clever and nonjudgmental in choosing goals that are reachable. Of course, there is nothing wrong with having big goals, since the overall goal is to learn an entire piece or pieces of music. However, if you are guided by your own desire to go into the flow state, you will never let the larger, more lofty goals discourage you or distract you even from what you are capable of doing one day at a time.

Another very important aspect of setting practice goals is to be absolutely clear about what you are able to accomplish given your perceived skill level and the time allotted. Having clear goals is one of the characteristics of being in the flow state. If you say to yourself, "I'm pretty sure I can do this," when assessing your practice assignments for the next day, then it is quite likely that this is an improper goal. If, however, you end up saying to yourself, "I will first practice this portion by portion until the entire segment is under my belt," then you have chosen a goal that you will most likely be successful in reaching.

THE FLOW LITMUS TEST

My doctoral research confirmed that when learning takes place while the pianist is in flow, confidence is sure to emerge. If your desire is to enjoy the optimal learning experience that flow practicing engenders, then it is essential that you recognize when flow is taking place. While reading this book, I'm sure at some point, you may have asked, "How else can I be sure that flow is taking place?" In fact, there are definite indicators that may help you answer this perplexing question. In her discussion of the flow state among children engaged in musical activities, Lori Custodero (2005) of Teachers College, Columbia University, described six behavioral indicators of flow:

1. Self-assignment
2. Self-correction
3. Deliberate gesture
4. Anticipation
5. Expansion
6. Extension

The presence or absence of these indicators will provide you with insight into whether you are engaging in flow practicing.

Self-Assignment

According to Custodero, the first flow indicator, self-assignment, is "associated with a sense of potential control" (2005). In the earlier discussions of the Beethoven German Dance and the Chopin Waltz, I asked that you not attempt to learn a practice unit that did not match your perceived skill level. Self-assignment is inherent in your behavior of choosing a segment to work on in a given practice session. It is also present in the segmenting that you do on your own. You have been instructed from the beginning to choose, or self-assign, appropriate segments on which to work, that is, segments for which challenge and skill are well matched. In response to this directive, you may find yourself becoming more adept at identifying and choosing to work on appropriate segments that have the potential of leading to flow, enjoyment, short-term mastery of the segment, intermediate-term mastery of a larger section, and long-term mastery of the entire piece.

Self-assigning appropriate segments focuses your attention on your skill level in relation to the actions to be learned. It also results in an ever-improving ability to assess both your skill level and the challenge level of the task at hand, a wonderful aptitude to acquire. Your going into the flow state is contingent on your ability to assess your own skill level before choosing a segment for which enjoyment, flow, or mastery (or ideally all three) is possible. You are also strongly urged to avoid choosing to work on segments that might give rise to frustration, anxiety, or boredom. Thus, your success is very much linked to a willingness and ability to scan the musical landscape in order to determine the segments that may provide the greatest potential for success or control, which, as we have seen, is an important flow characteristic.

Self-assignment of segments also can become a way for you to manage the risks associated with learning new skills. You may not realize it, but learning often coincides with a risk of failure, as you, the learner, attempt to make sense of each new practice segment. People who are timid about taking risks often find it difficult even to try because of the risk of failure. By choosing segments that provide the potential for learning in an enjoyable manner, this risk is lessened greatly, since risk has been replaced by potential enjoyment. You will find that the greatest successes occur when you choose segments that seem appropriate with regard to mastery and the potential for enjoyment.

Self-Correction

The second challenge-seeking indicator of flow identified by Custodero is self-correction. Correcting ourselves is often painful, as we have to admit that we have fallen short of our desired goal. If, however, you mindfully view the process of self-correction as a by-product of curiosity, you will be on the road to removing the impediments and negative associations that often accompany self-correction. To illustrate this point, I am reminded of Dan, a scientist and a good friend of mine, who in the early days of the computer (I believe I had a Commodore 64 back then) was able to place a positive spin on the most vexing complexities associated with learning "computerese" (which is how proficiency on the computer was thought of in those halcyon years). There was an enormous learning curve that needed to be experienced before one was able to start working at all with the computer. Every time we would come to another problem, I would feel massive frustration emerging inside. My friend, nonplussed and exuding confidence and curiosity, would exclaim "Fascinating!" every time one of these annoying moments would occur. The first couple of times he said this, I thought he was joking. However, after about the third or fourth utterance, I realized that he was quite serious and that he found such issues to be not frustrating but indeed both interesting and challenging. After a while, my own level of frustration diminished greatly as I began to take on his way of looking at things.

If we view the process of self-correction as an indictment of our own disabilities regarding practicing, we will develop a negative association toward this very necessary process. If, however, we simply say "Fascinating!" every time we come across a challenge no matter how big or small, like the eager traveler embarking on new and exciting adventures, we will become increasingly willing to delve deeply into and face the challenges that will occur. This fascination will lead you to modify your practicing in ways we have already discussed and will help you realize that almost all challenges have a solution. The desire to apply the "phases of learning" technique of going from the cognitive through the associative and ultimately to the autonomous stage will help you select and practice specific segments in which challenge and skill are closely matched.

The process of self-correcting and the flow characteristic of having clear goals go hand in hand. Being clear about your intentions on your way to mastery should give rise to viewing self-correction not as a possible indication of a deficiency or a personal flaw but as an interesting and necessary component of learning. Self-correction suggests the process of two of the characteristic elements of flow: perception of clear goals and reception of immediate feedback. Thus, learning in the manner advocated in this book will promote self-correction leading to mastery. In contrast, the least successful students tend to move on before mastery takes place and are typically less willing to self-correct in a manner that leads to mastery. Coupled with this is a tendency to misevaluate their level of skill, consistently overestimating the phase of learning that had been reached earlier on given segments. Here again, we see the relationship among mindfulness, accurate self-monitoring, and self-correction.

When we self-correct, we must be absolutely honest about our skill level, our musical intentions, and whether we have matched the two. It is important to be inspired by this process, understanding that all of your musical goals are attainable. The way forward is an adventure and worthy of your continuous fascination.

Deliberate Gesture

As you progress from the cognitive stage or the low associative stage (little automaticity, great deal of planning) to the high associative stage (almost entirely autonomous, very little planning) and beyond to the autonomous stage, your tone will become stronger as your gestures became increasingly sure and focused. This phenomenon, known as deliberate gesture, is another of the challenge-seeking indicators identified by Custodero. As you ascend in mastery and as you learn to use *only* those muscles essential to the task, your gestures will simply become more sure and confident. Your kinesthetic intelligence regarding each excerpt will strengthen. Assessing your progress through this lens will help you understand whether control is actually taking place. Ask yourself if there is any confusion regarding fingering, arm angles, posture, or any other slight physical awkwardness. If the answer is yes, modify the unit if you must in order to stay fascinated, and forge forward until even the slightest discomfort or physical tentativeness disappears.

Anticipation

You will also find as you progress that success leads to more success. Gaining confidence in your ability to learn will engender positive expectations for learning. Anticipating positive outcomes will add to enjoyment and learning efficacy. This will encourage you to seek even more success by practicing more often and for longer periods. Thus, anticipation, or actually looking forward to practicing, is a strong indicator of the presence of flow.

Expansion

As the excerpts become stronger and as self-correction leads to deliberate gesture and anticipation, you should observe the emergence of your unique musical spirit as exemplified by subtle changes in dynamics, expression, balance between the two hands, tempo fluctuations, and musical character. This gradual expansion of the technical toward the artistry of music making will emerge as your desire and enjoyment of the music lead you deeper into the flow state. A further manifestation of expansion occurs when you break down or combine segments in novel ways to further the goal of mastering larger portions of each piece.

Extension

The flow indicator of extension will also be present as small practice units gradually become larger, as success leads to success and as enjoyment and mastery increase. When practicing in this fashion, you will most likely experience so much enjoyment from your practice sessions that you will find yourself practicing for longer periods than you had anticipated, even losing track of time while you practice. Again, success leads to success, and flow leads to a desire for more flow which, again, will lead to greater time on task.

In order to ascertain your flow state with greater certainty, try asking yourself the following questions, presented along with the corresponding flow indicators.

1. Self-Assignment

Are you flexible regarding the excerpts you choose for learning, or are you rigidly sticking to a chronological plan of learning? The chronological plan is indicative of a mindless approach to learning. Remember that the desire is always to match skill and challenge, so a chronological approach is sure to present challenges that are either simply too easy or too difficult for maintaining flow. In addition, ask yourself if you are rigidly sticking to a plan whereby you attempt to learn excerpts of similar length. Since some excerpts are simple, your skill level may be sufficient to take several measures with hands together. On the other hand, the opposite may be true in the case of phrases of great difficulty. In order to avoid frustration in such a case, it may be necessary to take half a measure with hands separately. Flexibility in self-assignment is crucial to flow.

2. Self-Correction

Are you annoyed at yourself when you correct a mistake? Do you sometimes put yourself down with such utterances as "I must be stupid" or "I'm better than this—this shouldn't be so hard"? The best antidote to this antiflow thinking is to reframe the process by inserting the word *fascinating.* In fact, overcoming the myriad challenges of learning music is a fascinating journey worthy of your constant, (dare I say it) almost child-like curiosity as you ponder all the physical and musical variables that will unlock the mysteries of a given excerpt, rendering it learnable. Curiosity is the key to self-correction and is crucial to flow.

3. Deliberate Gesture

Are your gestures sure and true? Is there any kinesthetic doubt as a result of your not being quite sure if you have the correct arm placement or angle? Is there any uncertainty about your balance or finger shape? If not, then you have attained deliberate gesture; when you are in flow, there is no doubt or tentativeness.

4. Anticipation

Over time, do you find yourself thinking about the piano and anticipating how wonderful your next session will be because of the enjoyment and productivity of your work at the piano? Do you ever say to yourself something like "Great! I'll be able to spend four or five uninterrupted hours today—can't wait"? Do you view such sessions as you would view something else pleasant such as going on vacation or out with friends? Such positive anticipation is a hallmark of flow practicing.

5. Expansion

How else can you practice a passage to make it your own? As I have often stated, the creation of appropriately challenging practice units and the ability to combine or chunk these together will develop gradually and emerge over time. As you get deeper and deeper into flow practicing, you will undoubt-edly learn to create and combine practice chunks in novel ways, which will gradually conform uniquely with your personality. This departure from the formulaic into the personal coincides with the flow characteristic of expan-sion. Expansion occurs when you are drawn deeper and deeper into the piece and through your imagination, modifying practice by means of:

a. Use of the metronome.
b. Blocking arpeggiated passages.
c. Combining contrapuntal voicing in novel ways (for instance, in a three-part invention, you could combine all the two-voice combinations).

d. Altering rhythms (for instance, you can practice a stream of sixteenth notes by placing a fermata over the first of four:

Then the second of four:

And so on.

e. Doubling the treble or bass line with both hands, thus experiencing both parts on the opposite side of the body and, for that matter, the brain, since both brain hemispheres will then receive the information. You may have heard that the left hand is connected to and informs the right hemisphere, while the right hand informs and is connected to the left hemisphere. If you learn both parts with both hands, you will strengthen the neural networks governing both hands, thus placing the information from both clefs in both hemispheres.

f. Practicing legato passages staccato and vice versa.

g. Singing one line while playing the other.

Creating creative procedures exemplified by expansion is indicative of flow practicing.

6. Extension

Does your practicing seem to lead to more and more time on task? Do you find yourself saying, "Is it my imagination, or am I in fact practicing longer? As I have said, as you engage in flow practicing, your sessions will tend to lengthen. This is a function of enjoyment and is quite normal. The more we like something, the more we want to do it.

MINDFUL PRACTICING: COMBINED SELF-ASSESSMENT AND MINDFULNESS

One positive benefit of attempting to achieve mastery via flow practicing is an increase in mindfulness during the learning process. In order to be successful in your efforts to master the piano via flow practicing, it will be necessary for you to become mindful of several aspects of your practice experience. First, you have to decide to dedicate yourself to practicing. In order to pick an appropriate segment, you have to be aware of your own ability in relation to the demands of the segment you are seeking to master. Then you have to determine which segment to work on at any given moment and when you should move from one segment to the next. This effort will require you to become further aware of your current skill level and of the level of effort required to master a segment.

Over time, flow practicing will help you become increasingly adept at mindfully ascertaining your abilities as you choose segments on which to work. You will also gain expertise in ascertaining the level of challenge of each practice unit so you can modify the challenge according to your skill level.

Brown and Ryan (2003) observe that when individuals approach tasks mindfully, they are attentive to what is happening from moment to moment. They are also aware of the relationship between the activities of the moment and the goal of their activity. They suggest that attention and awareness are constant features of normal functioning, but they also assert that consistent mindfulness leads to enhanced attention to current experience and present reality. Flow practicing is one example of eliciting enhanced attention. Langer (1997, 280) suggests that individuals who demonstrate mindfulness are engaging in a process of making "finer and finer distinctions." Flow practicing will also lead you to consistent improvement regarding judgments about what and how to practice. Moreover, in bringing your attention to bear on the practice activity of the moment, you will be led away from the automatic belief in the difficulty of the overall endeavor that is so common. In avoiding such a belief, you will enhance your motivation to work hard to achieve both your short-term and longer-term goals.

The idea that mindfulness will enable you to avoid experiencing a sense of futility or apprehension about the possibility of failure may be viewed as a mutually beneficial relationship. Shao and Skarlicki (2009) specifically note that anxiety tends to disrupt attention. Thus, freedom from apprehension and anxiety may be viewed as a product of mindfulness, and/or mindfulness may be viewed as a product of freedom from anxiety. Alternatively, both freedom from anxiety and mindfulness may emerge from flow practicing.

Moreover, intense focus on the moment is a characteristic of the flow state, the achievement of which is inherently rewarding. Flow practicing promotes mindfulness, and that mindfulness promotes ever-enhancing flow practicing, which leads to increased learning and enjoyment. It is equally true that effective practice habits tend to promote efficiency in achieving mastery, and enjoyment promotes an increase in practice activity, further enhancing achievement.

BEING A WONDERFUL PERFORMER

Will goal setting and goal accomplishment alone be sufficient to create the self-confidence necessary to be a wonderful pianist? It pains me to say this, but the short answer is not necessarily. In order to be a wonderful pianist who is capable of performing under any circumstances, it is necessary to develop the level of self-esteem or self-confidence that will enable you to say honestly to yourself that what you have accomplished is at such a high level of expertise that you are ready and even eager to share it with others. Achieving this level of expertise, of course, is the point of this book. We have been very careful in scaffolding ways to enable you to consistently enjoy the peak experience that accompanies the flow state time and time again. Consistently achieving this state while practicing will get your psyche used to the idea of the flow, which will render it more attainable when you perform. Therefore, the more often you achieve flow while practicing, the more likely you will be to go into flow while performing. Having said this, what else can the pianist do in order to make a lasting internal shift that results in the creation of the positive self-concept of a performer?

CONFIDENCE

The word *confidence* comes from the Latin *confidentia*, which in turn is a combination of *cum* ("with") and *fidere* ("to fully trust"). A person with confidence, therefore, is a person imbued with trust in her own or others' abilities. The individual who is confident carries with her the sense that she can rely on herself to do well. She has faith in the positive outcomes of her actions. In order to trust in positive outcomes, our inner being demands that this trust be based in something that is rock-solid. Practicing wonderfully and achieving wonderful accomplishments will not necessarily lead to the self-concept necessary to gain this rock-solid trust in ourselves, that is, self-confidence. Again, only we can give this to ourselves. But if practicing in flow is not sufficient, how do we systematically build ourselves so that our confidence is impermeable? It may help us to remember that all the great performers we have ever witnessed have been successful in achieving this state. How may we do this for ourselves?

MASTERY LEADING TO CONFIDENCE LEADING TO PERFORMANCE MASTERY

The element we are seeking when attempting to develop a rock-solid level of expertise and self-concept as a performer must be developed carefully. Accepting that all procedures and actions must lead to the flow state, we must apply this also to performance. The goal of our actions will therefore be to create a self-concept that will create full trust in our capability to perform.

Once mastery of a given piece of music has been fully accomplished, we are now at the threshold of being able to perform it. However, in most cases, it will become necessary to systematically address the fear that often accompanies public performance. Recall that when one is in the flow state, both worry and self-consciousness disappear. Recall also that it is a state of full concentration during which what you are doing and what you are thinking become one thing. Most important, remember that successful entrance into the flow state is dependent on your ability to match your performance skill with the performance challenge you have chosen. The implications of this can be extremely powerful; going into the flow state during performance will enable you to be the best you can possibly be. It will enable you to perform at your best.

If you are to access this state, then what you choose to play, where and for whom you choose to play it, and how long you choose to perform will all become extremely important variables for your consideration.

TRUSTING IN YOUR CAPACITIES

When he was a baby, my son's favorite bedtime story was *The Little Engine That Could*. Unless I read it at least a half-dozen times, sleep was impossible (for both of us). This much-loved children's book by Watty Piper tells the story of a determined little train attempting to climb a mountain against seemingly insurmountable odds. Piper beautifully captures the fully loaded train's titanic struggle, a struggle that was more than matched by his determination to get up the mountain. Apparently, the train, laden with a very heavy cargo, had never ascended this particular mountain before, so his determination was based on only one thing: his faith in his internal resources to make it up and over the top.

Have you ever been that train? Have you ever somehow gained the confidence to surmount a challenge for which no prior experience existed? It could be something as simple as walking to school for the first time, where you had to deal with the fear of getting lost or not arriving on time. Riding a bicycle, going on your first date, and starting college all contained the threat of a possible fall or rejection. How were you able to gain the internal resources to say, "I think I can"? In the case of all three examples, at what point did it become "I'm sure I can" or "Of course I can"?

Gaining resources in order to give rise to faith in success is what every performer needs at every stage of his or her development. The key to these stages will be to foster the emergence of flow in every one of them.

SYSTEMATICALLY DESENSITIZING YOURSELF TO PERFORMANCE ANXIETY

Few of us are born performers. Yet a desire to share what we have created is universal. This is probably true whether that outlet is cooking, painting, sculpting, dancing, acting, restoring '65 Corvettes, or any other form of creativity. While there are those who create for themselves alone, the vast majority of artists tend to wish to share their art with others. To state the obvious, if we, as pianists, are to share our art, we simply must perform.

In order to bolster our confidence, there are systematic steps that we can take in line with flow practicing that will gradually reduce performance anxiety. Unless your confidence begins to soar, perform the following steps one right after the other.

1. Play the Five-Marker Game

This is a favorite among my students. While practicing, see if you can play a given passage at least five times in a row to your artistic satisfaction. Be honest; if it is even slightly beneath your standards, then it behooves you to start again. This procedure was favored by no less a luminary than Franz Liszt, who would place a marble in a vase every time he played a passage or an entire piece up to his lofty standards. You might be curious to know how this addresses performance anxiety. Try it. You will most likely discover encroaching anxiety as you get closer to your last iteration. Successfully overcoming your anxiety when attempting the last marker will add to your confidence. However, after a couple of attempts, you may find that reaching five is not possible for you. In this case, ask yourself what is doable. Perhaps doing it four or only three times is still possible. I have a student who when asked how many successful repetitions he is capable of, unfailingly answers "Two." My reaction is always "OK, you're the boss." You will discover that two successful repetitions will gain you the confidence needed to do three. Three will lead to four and four to five.

It will be easy to apply this to the Beethoven German Dance in A Major, which we discussed in chapter 5:

German Dance

Ludwig van Beethoven (1770-1827)

Each line consists of two two-measure potential practice segments. Each segment may therefore be mastered in this manner. If this impresses you as being far too easy, then in order to maintain flow, it will be necessary to increase the challenge somewhat. In this case, instead of two measures, you may decide to practice an entire line.

2. Practice the Piece in Its Entirety via the Five-Marker Game

Once the small units have been mastered, it is possible to work on increasingly larger sections until the entire piece is learned. Consider again the German Dance. This piece is in the form of ABCD. It consists of four different four-measure phrases. Study each line until it can be played accurately and musically five times in a row. After all four lines have been learned separately, play the first two lines as a unit five times, accurately and musically, then do the same with the second phrase. In other words, treat the first half of the piece as one unit and the second half of the piece as a second unit. Finally, play the entire piece five times, accurately and musically. This procedure is best represented by a pyramid (see figure 7.1), in which the bottom row is divided into four triangles, each representing a phrase. The small diamonds represent each half of the piece, and the large diamond represents the piece in its entirety. Students who faithfully follow this procedure, or their own version of it, taking care to avoid mistakes, should be successful at mastering their music. They can achieve success because they have absorbed the piece in increasingly larger sections. Students who follow Liszt's procedure find that playing a measure, a phrase, or an entire piece perfectly five or more times in a row leads most often to eventual mastery.

Naturally, the more times you practice the piece via the five-marker game, the stronger it will be. Remember that you are attempting to move into the autonomous zone for the piece in its entirety. For some of you, that will mean doing each section more—perhaps many more—than five times. However, some of you may feel that counting successes actually has the effect of taking you out of flow because of the self-consciousness that may engender. If this is the case, I would recommend that you simply replace counting with the goal of moving into the autonomous zone with each practice fragment.

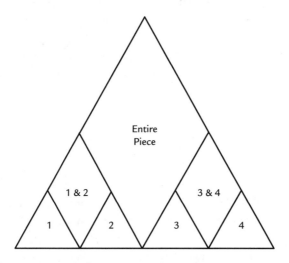

Figure 7.1 The practice pyramid

3. Play an Informal Rendition of a Passage or More for a Friend

After accomplishing steps 1 and/or 2, you may feel ready to play a portion of the piece for a friend. In order to keep it light and informal, you can invite the friend by saying something like "I really love this passage [or phrase or page or whatever amount feels friendly and doable]. Can I play it for you?" In this way, you are easing yourself into a situation in which the listener's expectations are pretty minimal. After several of these attempts with different people or even the same person, you may be ready and confident enough to play larger passages.

4. Perform a Passage or More for a Friend

Step three is decidedly informal, as the operative word is *play*, which not only connotes an informal rendering of your selection but also indicates that you are engaging in the activity as an amusement. When you tell a friend that you'd like to *perform* for him or her, the stakes are higher. You are implying that you are confident that you have something that is polished and ready to be heard by others. When you take this step, you are under no obligation to play an entire piece. If you are comfortable playing only one section, so be it. Confidence is gained not through failures but through successes. If your inner voice tells you that you're not quite sure if a portion of the piece is ready, then you should probably assume it is *not* ready and that to play it would be to court a situation in which you may not be successful. There is no reason you should put yourself through this. Naturally, there will be a gray area when you are not quite sure yet if you should perform it. If this is the case, I would recommend going back to steps 1 and 2 and even 3 in order to gain the confidence necessary for you to become the "Little Engine That Could" who had such a positive anticipation of the future that he was able to say, "I think I can." Over time, you will learn when your level of confidence is sufficient to support the next and future steps.

5. Perform the Entire Piece for a Friend or Two

After successfully accomplishing several or all of the previous steps, you may feel ready to perform the entire piece. I would suggest that you choose your audience carefully, making sure that the person or persons you play for are sympathetic and supportive. If you approach this as a means of sharing the way you would share your cooking, your hospitality, or any other gift, then your ego, with its cravings for approval, is not involved. I am reminded of a wonderful story I heard about thirty-five years ago while taking a lesson from the esteemed piano teacher Vlazia Mashke at her spacious and marvelous apartment on the Upper West Side of Manhattan. As a very young woman, Mashke (who at the time of my lesson was quite elderly) had attended a recital at Carnegie Hall by the legendary pianist Vladimir de Pachmann. Her story went something like this: "He was a peculiar sort—full of generosity of spirit and surprises. Going to one of his concerts was always an event. Once in a while, this generosity got a bit out of hand, in my opinion. De Pachmann had just finished playing a set of Rachmaninoff Preludes. After the final Prelude, he turned to the person in the first row and exclaimed, 'Wasn't that beautiful? Thank you for listening!' I believe the astonished listener said something along the lines of 'The pleasure was all mine.'" With her story, my teacher had made it clear that she felt that de Pachmann's playing was given as a gift to the audience and that I should follow his example, in that music, when given as a gift, benefits both listener and performer. The legendary pianist Artur Rubinstein was similar in his demeanor and personality. Franz Mohr, the legendary concert piano tuner for Steinway, said this about Rubinstein: "People really loved Artur Rubinstein, because he loved people. Whenever people sought his autograph, on the street or on a plane or train, he would always stop and chat with them. . . . He always had time for people" (Mohr and Schaefer 1998, 50). As a young person, I idolized Rubinstein. He had the uncanny ability to make your feel special and transformed. His great love of humanity poured out of every note.

If you approach music making as an act of love, you will find your own trepidations diminished greatly, for you will have removed one of the greatest impediments to performing: trying to prove yourself. There's a saying that was always repeated by radio psychologist David Viscott; I print it at the bottom of all my recital programs: "Life gives life to those who give to life." This is really what you are doing when you perform.

6. Perform for a Select Audience

Having proceeded through the previous steps, you are now ready to perform confidently for larger gatherings of people. Remember always that no matter who is in the audience, you are giving them a gift. Released from the need to prove yourself, you will find that the tempos you choose are not at your extreme but are just beneath them. This sometimes is a hard notion for young people to grasp, since they often equate quality with speed. They often think, without realizing it, that the faster they play, the better. Nothing could be farther from the truth. There is an enormous fluctuation in tempi, often by the same pianists, with the same piece. If we are to make sure that we go into flow, then we must choose an interpretation that is just below or commensurate with our skill level. This means to stay within ourselves and not attempt to do more than we are capable of doing.

It is advisable to select your own audience for this attempt. When choosing, ask yourself if the people are supportive of your efforts and if they have an ability to be nurturing.

7. Perform for the Public

Having gone through the previous steps, you should now have the courage to play for the general public. If, in fact, you have scaffolded your performance challenges carefully, you are probably ready. But you really must be honest with yourself. Implementing each of these steps involves risk and delving into the unknown. If you have truly and honestly done the hard work necessary, if you have discovered enjoyment in all of these steps, and if these steps have been accomplished in the psychological state of flow, then most likely you are ready. The word *courage* has as its root the French word *coeur*, or "heart." Accomplishing the preceding steps will most likely provide you with the necessary heart to attempt this exciting risk. Remember that performance is a gift—just go for it.

SUMMARY

It should be obvious that flow practicing can provide you with an enormous overall benefit as the negative is eliminated and the various positive benefits of mindfulness, accomplishment, enjoyment, imagination, confidence, and courage are greatly enhanced and developed over time. The expansion of these positive advantages will have a profound effect on your performance well-being. Since your practice sessions will be devoid of self-doubt and negative thinking, every effort will be imbued with positive associations. As you will be practicing with a positive mind, so will you perform with a positive mind. As you scaffold your performance experiences through the gradual building of performance challenges, you should also see your performance confidence gradually building. Dread of the stage will be replaced by positive expectation, perhaps even eagerness to perform. Like the beautiful butterfly freshly emerged from its cocoon, the positive pianist will be ready to fly and soar.

CHAPTER 8

Teaching to Flow

This book is primarily addressed to students learning to play the piano. The principles I've described also pertain, of course, to teachers who wish to provide assignments and create conditions for evoking the flow state in their students. What has not yet been discussed, however, is the fact that the teacher will be far more effective when flow takes place during the lesson itself.

As a result of both participating in and frequently discussing flow-enhancing activities with your students, you should find that they will go into the flow state with greater frequency. You should also find that you yourself may be able to access this state while teaching and that you will often be able to be "in the moment." Research has demonstrated, and experience tells us, that emotions are contagious (Bakker 2005) and that positive and negative emotions can cross over from one person to another. It is therefore reasonable to assume that teachers in flow have a far greater chance of inducing the same response in their students. Teachers in flow tend not to be judgmental, since they have a greater propensity for viewing teaching difficulties as challenges rather than failures. Bakker writes:

> The more flow experiences music teachers reported, the higher the frequency of comparable experiences among their students. This finding is in line with emotional contagion theory [Hatfield, Cacioppo, and Rapson 1994], and is one of the first demonstrations in field research that positive emotions may crossover from one person to another [Westman 2001]. The correlational analysis suggested that, in particular, teachers' intrinsic work motivation was related to flow experienced by students. . . . In addition, music teachers' and students' absorption and enjoyment also showed positive relationships, and enjoyment had the highest loading on the latent variable flow in the SEM-analyses. Thus,

these results suggest that students caught the flow experience of their teachers in a partly conscious and partly unconscious way. The crossover process may include the automatic imitation of a cheerful and happy teacher, but also the more conscious crossover of teachers' dedication to their work [cf. Hatfield, Cacioppo, and Rapson 1994]. In addition, motivated teachers probably put more effort and energy in the search for nice and suitable music for the students; they presumably have a more positive attitude toward work that motivates their students to concentrate during the music lesson and to perform well.

(Bakker 2005, 38)

Teachers who experience peak experience while teaching engender the same in their students.

When confronted with the inevitable problems that arise during a private (or even group) lesson, such teachers tend to become curious rather than negative. For instance, they seldom resort to the commonly heard "You need to practice harder" in addressing pianistic issues. They certainly do not resort to overt or even subtle put-downs or insults. This curiosity can be used to fuel a creative solution that will in turn become a permanent part of the teacher's repertoire of solutions or "bag of tricks." A teacher in flow will tend to view student dilemmas as an opportunity to become a better teacher. In addition, teachers who seek to teach to flow tend to view the entire process of teaching as one of challenge and seem better able to intuit student learning capacities and desires.

Like a rock climber seeking the challenge of a perfect hill or a skier searching for the perfect run, a teacher who seeks flow is more willing to view each teaching situation as an opportunity for increasing teaching skills and thus will choose materials, activities, and a pedagogical presentation that will challenge students to their optimal skill level. Teachers who teach to flow tend to create an atmosphere in which learning becomes a mutual journey. They become far more spontaneous, curious, and creative. In this environment, it will often be hard to know where the teacher ends and the student begins, as students and teacher become involved in the inspiring dance of learning in which such distinctions are blurred. Tapping into this wonderful stream of creative consciousness should enable both teacher and student to look forward to being in each other's company and thus should give new meaning to teaching piano class. My own exploration into the phenomenon of teaching to flow may be illustrated by the following incident that took place while I was teaching a college piano class.

Approximately halfway through a recent semester, it occurred to me that I had not yet worked on scales with the freshman secondary piano class, a course for vocalists needing to improve their keyboard proficiency. I had delayed this very important subject because teaching scales is my least favorite part of the curriculum, a sentiment also shared by most students, who seem to find learning scales both tedious and boring. As a result, their efforts often end up being unmusical, inaccurate in fingering, and plagued by wrong notes. Because of our mutual dislike of scales, I had procrastinated for almost half a semester. However, this time, I endeavored to find a way to make scales both interesting and enjoyable. I was intent on not repeating the past boring procedure.

I recalled that in one of my doctoral classes at Teachers College, Columbia University, I had watched a video of a cello lesson in which the teacher taught the scale through call-and-response improvisation. Using varied articulations and rhythms, he would play a portion of the scale and then ask the student to repeat. After a while, the leader and follower roles changed, with the student leading the improvisation. I found the results to be musical and engaging and decided to try to adapt this approach with my own piano class.

Beginning with the A-major scale and using fingers 1, 2, and 3, I improvised a one-measure phrase on the notes A, B, and C-sharp. Asking the students to echo this, I repeated these three notes using different rhythms and articulations. Using fingers 1, 2, 3, and 4 and then 1 again, I repeated this approach with the last five notes of the scale: D, E, F-sharp, G-sharp, and A. Again, the students echoed me. I then extended my improvisations to include all eight notes. The students echoed me again. Since I had to include all eight notes in one measure, the note values became smaller, and the students had to play faster. Trying to make the improvisations as interesting as possible, I was careful to vary both the rhythm and the articulation. The students imitated.

This procedure went on for about ten minutes, until we had thoroughly explored the scale two octaves up and down with both hands. I followed this approach by asking the students to improvise on their own. Interestingly, the students had seemed to learn the scale rather effortlessly; they played with accuracy and musicality, with tone that was robust and confident. Equally impressive was the fact that time seemed to be flying (the ten minutes really seemed like one), and the looks in the eyes of the students indicated that they were enjoying the experience. We were all very impressed that this new approach to learning the A-major scale had been musical, enjoyable, and, judging from the vastly increased accuracy, which never diminished for the rest of the semester, highly effective.

This story demonstrates how one of the typical skills we teach on a regular basis, playing scales, can be revitalized, energized, and simultaneously delivered in a more effective manner by attempting to create conditions whereby student concentration and enjoyment are enhanced.

Teaching to flow will call upon you to become consistently mindful of not only what you are asking of your students but also what you are asking of yourself. If you take on the teaching challenge of asking a student to do something within the lesson that he or she is incapable of doing, you are setting up a situation that is potentially frustrating for both of you. If your goal is to be the best teacher you can be and to create optimal experiences for teaching, then demanding too much of the student's present skill level, of course, is counterproductive.

PSYCHIC ENTROPY IN THE LESSON

All of us can undoubtedly recall lessons that were either frustrating or anxiety-provoking. Such an atmosphere undermines the educational process, resulting in a lowering rather than a raising of student ability.

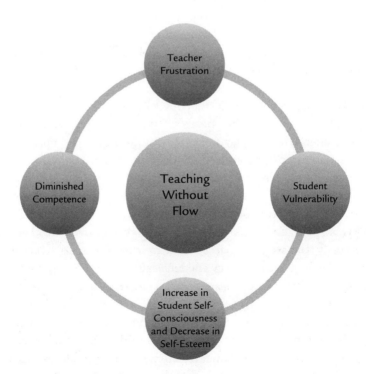

Figure 8.1 Teaching without flow

A negative self-perpetuating cycle may emerge, endangering the effectiveness of the lesson (see figure 8.1).

If students are caught up in such a cycle, there is little they can do to extricate themselves from the situation. In a worst-case scenario, this teaching style will probably result in a negative effect on the student's overall self-esteem and well-being, leading to further diminishment of skills on the piano and possibly even in everyday life. When there is an absence of flow, psychic dissonance can occur, in which conflicting thoughts or negative emotions interfere with the learning process. This inner conflict creates stress and thus slows down learning. Called psychic entropy, it is described as follows by Csikszentmihalyi:

> Whenever information disrupts consciousness by threatening its goals we have a condition of inner disorder, or psychic entropy, a disorganization of the self that impairs its effectiveness. Prolonged experiences of this kind can weaken the self to the point that it is no longer able to invest attention and pursue its goals. (1990, 37)

So, if experiences can in fact "weaken the self to the point that it is no longer able to invest attention and pursue its goals," psychic entropy is thus responsible for low motivation, bad moods, passivity, and unfocused attention (Price 2001; Persall 2003). However, we all face the session-to-session challenges of what to do when confronted with the numerous rhythmic, technical, musical, stylistic, and even psychological issues that arise in every lesson.

CREATIVITY AND OPENNESS IN THE LESSON

Over the years, I have experienced that one of the most challenging passages involving rhythm, style, interpretation, and technique occurs in the sixth measure of Debussy's First Arabesque. Generally, the student, who is typically about thirteen to fifteen years old and quite musical, has heard the piece and has asked me, or even begged me, to allow him or her to learn it. In fact, knowing the issues that will occur in that infamous measure 6, I normally will not assign this piece unless there is a strong desire on the part of the student to learn it. Strong initial student motivation is a great indicator of student readiness for difficult music.

Measure 6 has special issues that, unless dealt with carefully, may elicit an unmusical outcome. The passage must exhibit an impressionistic fluency yet retain absolute rhythmic precision. This will often be among the student's initial attempts at playing two against three, increasing the challenge considerably. Generally, students are able to play each hand musically when playing hands-separate. It is in putting it together that the difficulties arise. It has been my experience that few students are able to initially contend with this challenge:

Often, the result is either a Latin feel, in which, in order to keep the left hand's eighth notes even, the triplet becomes something along the lines of

or vice versa, in which the student, in his or her desire to keep the right hand accurate, will distort the left hand:

In the first example, the student distorts the duplets to accommodate the triplet, and in the second example, the opposite occurs The standard way of teaching this might be to have the student tap according to the rhythm:

This solution, however, does not take into account the eighth notes at the start of the measure in the left hand. It will solve the rhythmic issues for the next four twos against threes, but the result will most likely be rhythmically inflexible, harsh, and devoid of nuance:

Such results will try the patience of any well-meaning teacher.

I'm sure you will agree that a situation like this has the potential to be frustrating for both teacher and student. The great question then becomes how one retains the French nuanced and improvisatory feel while retaining the correct mathematical ratios. This is the kind of challenge that involves the whole person, not just the piano-playing mechanism of the body. Since we want to imbue the student with a coordinated feel for the rhythm, the solution entails holistically teaching the entire body. Naturally, this type of teaching is typically outside most piano teachers' range of interventions. However, it is just this kind of "out of the box" thinking that is required to master this challenge.

The following lesson plan may help with this and similar passages. If internalized well, it will increase the coordination between limbs and the brain's two hemispheres. You'll need some space to do this. Before going on to each new step, each step must reach the autonomous phase, so it may take several days to become comfortable. Stick with the plan, and above all, have fun.

1. Step the triplets in a nonlinear, dancelike, musical fashion. Don't be afraid to explore the space behind you and to the side. Have fun, and improvise, making sure that you attain a somewhat circular yet free rendering of this rhythm. Once this step is comfortable, move on to step 2.
2. Clap even eighths in front of you but in different places in your immediate surroundings. Pretend that the space in front of you is filled with fireflies that you are gently trying to catch and hold for only a second. Be sure not to clap too hard. (Aside from the obvious harm that would befall the imaginary firefly, clapping too hard will create a harsh, unnuanced tone.)
3. Alternate between the two. When you are able to go smoothly from one activity to the other without any "hiccups," move to step 4.
4. Try combining both activities at the same time according to the following rhythm (make sure that "catch," "fi," and "fly" are in your feet,

while "catch" and "re" are in the hands). To experience the proper nuance, make sure that you step in a dancelike, nonlinear way. It is also important that the claps remain gentle and in different places in front of you.

Catch fi - re - fly Catch fi - re - fly Catch fi - re - fly Catch fi - re - fly

Once the above procedure is comfortable, graceful, and fun, then you have successfully internalized the basics of this rhythmic challenge of three against two. However, in order to learn it fully so that it may be possible to transfer it to the piano, it is essential that you also be able to do the opposite, which is to place the duplets in the feet while placing the triplets in the hands, using the following steps:

5. Try step 1 above with your hands (that is, clap in a triplet rhythm as you "catch fireflies"). Remember that each part of the triplet should be in a different place and that the claps need to be gentle.
6. Now walk in the duplet rhythm of step 2. Even though this a duplet, it is again important that it not be performed in a linear fashion. The shifts in weight that occur when you change direction will keep the activity challenging and will help maintain your interest.
7. Combine both stages (walking duplets and clapping triplets). This step is by far the hardest, as there will be a temptation to "insert" the second note of the triplet between the two notes of the duplet instead of just before it. This step needs to be practiced until it can be executed with grace and nuance.
8. Alternate the roles of the hands and the feet until you can smoothly and musically go back and forth between the two patterns described.

Once this exercise has become effortless and graceful, try playing the Arabesque. Regardless of how familiar you may have been with this piece already, I'm sure you will note an enhancement in the flexibility and independence of the rhythm between the two hands.

You may have noticed that you entered the state of flow while doing the activity above. Applying this type of "away from the keyboard" approach for learning passages such as this is a wonderful way to enhance your students' interest, while at the same time providing a kinesthetic solution to problems involving rhythm and coordination. In addition, activities like this are enjoyable and highly productive (think of the possibilities when teaching baroque and classical dances, jazz, pop, and other movement-oriented piano pieces).

CHOOSING LESSON GOALS WISELY

As I have said, teaching to flow involves your ability to ascertain whether the teaching goals you are trying to accomplish are actually doable during the lesson. If you monitor your own reactions, you will get a clue about how well you have chosen. If you are feeling frustrated, then the task you are asking your student to accomplish is most likely far too complex or difficult to be accomplished in the time allotted (in the case of boredom or apathy, it is just the opposite). For both of your sakes, it is therefore important for you to develop the ability to provide challenges both at and away from the piano that are well matched to the student's ability and accomplishable during the lesson. Giving the student the experience of really mastering a passage of music (no matter the size) during the lesson will provide him or her with a model that can be replicated at home or in the practice room.

Naturally, the approach of teaching to flow is student-oriented rather than teacher-oriented. Teachers who come to each lesson with a rigid notion of how a piece should be played or with an approach that leaves no room for student individuality will not be successful in teaching lessons that result in flow. There are firm philosophical underpinnings that support this notion. American educational psychologist Jerome Bruner maintains that learning should be goal-directed and driven by curiosity. This idea charges the teacher with the need to probe and inquire into the student's personality and interests to best discover what and how the student can be motivated to learn. Decisions as diverse as repertory choices, touch, technique, and tone all will emerge organically if the teacher possesses the curiosity to create a lesson ambience in which the student may become a vested learner or an agent in his or her own learning.

It is hard to believe, but even today, the old-fashioned pedagogical strategy of using one technical approach for all students or teaching through teacher demonstration and student imitation persists today (Camp 1992). This is true despite the exhortations of one of the most famous piano teachers in history. More than one hundred years ago, the great Theodor Leschetizky stated:

> One learns from every new pupil, the untalented as well as the talented. . . . Don't have a method; it is far better to leave your mind blank for the pupil to fill

in. You will discover more easily, in this way, what he needs. Even in technique
it is impossible to have a method, for every hand is different.

(quoted in Uszler, Gordon, and McBride-Smith 2000, 293)

Research has also revealed that a majority of lesson time is spent on
teacher talk rather than student talk (Kostka 1984). Of course, such an
approach prevents students from expressing and verbally exploring issues
pertaining to their own development.

Teaching to flow will place less pressure on you as the teacher, since
the responsibility for student growth will be shared equally by you and
the student. Teaching to flow, with its emphasis on intrinsic motivation, will enable the student to become mindful of his or her work while
in your presence and will enable you to ask questions such as "Which
part of the passage did you enjoy the most?" or "There were sections
of the page that were just gorgeous. Can you tell me where you think
they occurred? What was it that made your playing so rich and beautiful
here? That was so special." Such an inquiry-based approach will send the
message that you respect the student as an emerging artist and that the
lesson is a safe environment for the mutual exploration of music. If you
listen carefully, you may even learn what kind of muse seems to sing to
your student.

TEACHING THE STUDENT AS A PASSIONATE
EMERGING ARTIST

Many years ago, while attending the Manhattan School of Music, I had
the opportunity to become friendly with many developing piano vir-
tuosos. Invariably, all the students possessed technique that was
astonishing in its power and speed. However, only a few students
were able to play in a transcendent manner that left you tingling.
Being in such a milieu among dozens of pianists enabled me to recognize the teachers who were responsible for training both the transcendent and the nontranscendent students. The students who were
less than transcendent all played similarly, and it was difficult to dis-
tinguish them from their own teachers. It was obvious that the type
of teaching that was taking place with this kind of student was the
imitative "this is how it's done" style. The student's musical soul was
not taken into consideration or nurtured. Students from that and
similar studios all became adept at imitation but not at expressing

something that was unique. Each piece was performed in a safe and correct style with little risk taking or spontaneity.

The students who had the ability to play transcendentally, however, had all started with teachers who were willing to explore student preferences and nurture their spirit. Students from teachers such as these were not always spot-on stylistically. Often, they might be accused of being overly effusive as they explored the outer reaches of tempo, interpretation, and spirituality. The teachers of these students allowed them to have unique voices, even though taking such a risk might result in criticism from colleagues. Yet who among us would prefer to go to a stylistically correct but spiritless performance over one that was stylistically adventurous but contained the potential for transcendence?

Another incident illustrates this point. Several years after studying at the Manhattan School of Music, I was fortunate to study conducting at the Aspen Music Festival. The teacher, Murry Sidlin, who today maintains a very active and important conducting career, insisted that we never listen to recordings when learning a score. He felt that doing so would prevent us from delving deeply into the score and making our own decisions regarding interpretation, balance, tempo, and the myriad details necessary to perform a great work of orchestral music. I remember distinctly his exhorting us, "If you imitate Herbert von Karajan, Zubin Mehta, or Pierre Boulez, then who the hell needs you?" We would all agree that what makes music great is an unmatched interpretation that helps us gain insight into music or even into life in general. Imitation, therefore, is really unacceptable if we are trying to nurture artists.

Teaching to flow (see figure 8.2) will allow you to stay curious, fresh, and open to all students' ideas, thoughts, and struggles. It will enable you to experience yourself as a student and your student as the teacher, a role reversal that will allow for mutual respect.

Because of its open-ended possibilities, pursuing flow may at times feel risky. Yet truly there can be no triumph without risk. Taking the daily risk to practice, perform, and teach creatively toward flow will result in triumphs that will grow in magnitude over time. Flow is its own reward!

CODA

As we end this exploration together you may have begun to realize that genius itself depends on one's ability to consistently enter into flow. With these thoughts in mind I can think of no better way to conclude than

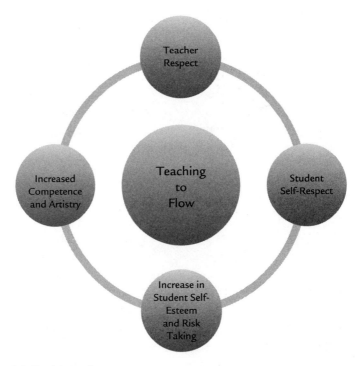

Figure 8.2 Teaching to flow

by leaving you with this inspiring observation from Paul Pearsall's *The Beethoven Factor*:

> Beethoven showed all the characteristics of someone who could enter a state of flow. His composing of his music was his form of a highly creative consciousness that allowed him to construe whatever happenned to him in such a way that he could become totally unaware of himself and his problems. He wrote to a friend, 'I live only in music, frequently working on three or four pieces simultaneously.' His deep despair over losing his hearing seemed to be overwhelmed by his ability to get into flow, to find total consuming happiness in his creative work.
>
> (Pearsall 2003, 161)

I would consider that the mission of this book has been fulfilled if as a result of reading it you would *never ever doubt your ability to enjoy both the powerful benefits of flow and the genius that flow can release over time.*

REFERENCES

Abell, Arthur M. 1987. *Talks with Great Composers*. New York: Philosophical Library.

Abuhamdeh, Sami, Mihaly Csikszentmihalyi, and Jeanne Nakamura. 2005. "Flow." In *Handbook of Competence and Motivation*, edited by Andrew J. Elliot and Carol S. Dweck, 508–608. New York: Guilford Press.

Amis, John. 2009. "In Tune with the Infinite." *Musical Opinion* 132 (July/August): 26.

Bakker, Arnold B. 2005. "Flow among Music Teachers and Their Students: The Crossover of Peak Experiences." *Journal of Vocational Behavior* 66: 26–44.

Brach, T. 2004. *Radical Acceptance: Embracing Your Life with the Heart of a Buddha*. New York: Bantam Books.

Brown, Brené. 2012. *Daring Greatly: How the Courage to Be Vulnerable Transforms the Way We Live, Love, Parent, and Lead*. New York: Gotham Books.

Brown, K. W., and Ryan, R. M. 2003. "The Benefits of Being Present: Mindfulness and Its Role in Psychological Well-being." *Journal of Personality and Social Psychology* 84(4): 822–848.

Cameron, Judy, and W. David Pierce. 2002. *Rewards and Intrinsic Motivation: Resolving the Controversy*. Westport, Conn.: Bergin & Garvey.

Camp, Max W. 1992. *Teaching Piano: The Synthesis of Mind, Ear, and Body*. Van Nuys, Calif.: Alfred.

Csikszentmihalyi, Mihaly. 1975. *Beyond Boredom and Anxiety*. San Francisco: Jossey-Bass.

——. 1990. *Flow: The Psychology of Optimal Experience*. New York: Harper & Row.

——. 1996. "Motivated Social Cognition: Principles of the Interface." In *Social Psychology: Handbook of Basic Principles*, edited by E. Tory Higgins and Arie W. Kruglanski, 493–520. New York: Guilford Press.

——. 1997. *Finding Flow: The Psychology of Engagement with Everyday Life*. New York: Basic Books.

——. 1997. "Happiness and Creativity: Going with the Flow." *The Futurist*, 31(5): SR8+.

Custodero, Lori A. 1997. "An Observational Study of Flow Experience in Young Children's Music Learning." Doctoral dissertation, University of Southern California, Los Angeles.

——. 1998. "Observing Flow in Young Children's Music Learning." *General Music Today* 12: 21–27.

——. 1999. "The Construction of Musical Understandings: The Flow-Cognition Interface" [extended abstract]. *Bulletin for the Council of Research in Music Education* 142: 79–80.

——. 2003a. "Perspectives on Challenge: A Longitudinal Investigation of Children's Music Learning." *Arts and Learning* 19: 23–53.

———. 2003b. "Seeking Challenge, Finding Skill: Flow Experience in Music Education." *Arts Education and Policy Review* 103: 3–9.

———. 2005. "Observable Indicators of Flow Experience: A Developmental Perspective of Musical Engagement in Young Children from Infancy to School Age." *Music Education Research* 7: 185–209.

Custodero, Lori A., and Patricia A. St. John. 2007. "Actions Speak: Lessons Learned from the Systematic Observation of Flow Experience in Young Children's Music Making." In *Listen to Their Voices: Research and Practice in Early Childhood Music*, edited by Katharine Smithrim and Rena Upitis, 2–18. Toronto: Canadian Music Educators' Association.

Deci, Edward L., and Richard M. Ryan. 1980. "Self-Determination Theory: When Mind Mediates Behavior." *Journal of Mind and Behavior* 1: 33–43.

———. 1984. *Intrinsic Motivation and Self-Determination in Human Behavior.* New York: Plenum.

———. 2000. "Intrinsic and Extrinsic Motivations: Classic Definitions and New Directions." *Contemporary Educational Psychology* 25: 54–67.

Ericsson, K. Anders. 2000. "Expert Performance and Deliberate Practice: An Updated Excerpt from Ericsson (2000)." *Expertise.* http://www.psy.fsu.edu/faculty/ericsson/ericsson.exp.perf.html.

Ehrlich, D. 1997. *Inside the Music: Conversations with Contemporary Musicians about Spirituality, Creativity, and Consciousness.* Boston: Shambala.

Evans, Allan. 2009. *Ignaz Friedman: Romantic Master Pianist.* Bloomington, Ind.: Indiana University Press.

Fitts, Paul M., and Michael I. Posner. 1967. *Human Performance.* Belmont, Calif.: Brooks/Cole.

Gallwey, W. Timothy. 2009. *The Inner Game of Golf,* rev. ed. New York: Random House.

Gladwell, M. 2008. *Outliers: The Story of Success.* New York: Little Brown and Co.

Gobet, F., P.C.R. Lane, S. Croker, et al. 2001. "Chunking Mechanisms in Human Learning." *Trends in Cognitive Science* 5: 236–243.

Harlow, H. F., M. K. Harlow, and D. R. Meyer. 1950. "Learning Motivated by a Manipulation Drive." *Journal of Experimental Psychology* 40: 228–234.

Hatfield, Elaine, John T. Cacioppo, and Richard L. Rapson. 1994. *Emotional Contagion.* New York: Cambridge University Press.

Kostka, Marilyn J. 1984. "An Investigation of Reinforcements, Time Use, and Student Attentiveness in Piano Lessons." *Journal of Research in Music Education* 32: 113–22.

Lang, L., and D. Ritz. 2008. *Journey of a Thousand Miles: My Story.* New York: Spiegel & Grau.

Langer, Ellen J. 1997. *The Power of Mindful Learning.* Reading, Mass.: Addison-Wesley.

Martin, Rosy. 1986. "Phototherapy: The School Photograph (Happy Days Are Here Again)." In *Photography/Politics: Two,* edited by Patricia Holland, Jo Spence, and Simon Watney, 40–42. London: Comedia/Photography Workshop.

Mohr, F., and E. Schaeffer. 1996. *My Life with the Great Pianists.* Grand Rapids, Mich.: Baker Books.

Pearsall, P. (2003). *The Beethoven Factor: The New Positive Psychology of Hardiness, Happiness, Healing, and Hope.* Charlottesville, VA: Hampton Roads Pub. Co.

Pink, Daniel H. 2009. *Drive: The Surprising Truth about What Motivates Us.* New York: Penguin.

Price, S. (2001). "Philosophical Challenges from Students: 'What's the bottom line?'" Piano Pedagogy Forum, http://www.music.sc.edu/ea/keyboard/PPF/4.2/4.2.PPFgp.html.

Shao, R., and D. P. Skarlicki. 2009. "The Role of Mindfulness in Predicting Individual Performance." *Canadian Journal of Behavioural Science* 41(4): 195.

Simon, Cecelia Capuzzi. 2005. "Mr. Mindfulness: Living in the Moment Is Tough, Even for the Idea's Leading Exponent: Just Ask Jon Kabat-Zinn." *Washington Post*, July 12, F1.

Stravinsky, Igor, and Robert Craft. 1962. *Expositions and Developments*. Garden City, N.Y.: Doubleday.

Uszler, Marienne, Stewart Gordon, and Scott McBride-Smith. *The Well-Tempered Keyboard Teacher*, 2d ed. Belmont, Calif.: Wadsworth Group/Thomson Learning.

Westman, Mina. 2001. "Stress and Strain Crossover." *Human Relations* 54: 717–51.

INDEX